Reflective Meditations Trilogy:
Understanding My Authentic Self
Believing in Myself
Loving Myself
Plus
Understanding My Boundaries

Script and photography by
Audrey Tait, MS

Published by Inspirational Insights Counselling, Inc.

Library and Archives Canada Cataloguing in Publication

Tait, Audrey, 1959-, author, photographer
Reflective meditations trilogy / script and photography by
Audrey Tait, MS.

Includes index.
Contents: [Trilogy 1] Understanding my trauma; Healing my
trauma; Letting go--forgiveness! -- [trilogy 2] Understanding
my authentic self; Believing in myself; Loving myself; Understanding my boundaries.
Issued in print and electronic formats.
ISBN 978-0-9952326-6-2 (trilogy 1 : softcover).
--ISBN 978-0-9952326-8-6 (trilogy 2 : softcover).
--ISBN 978-0-9952326-7-9 (trilogy 1 : EPUB).
--ISBN 978-0-9952326-9-3 (trilogy 2 : EPUB)

1. Psychic trauma. 2. Self-acceptance. 3. Meditation. I. Title.

BF575.S37T35 2017. 158.1. C2017-903422-7
C2017-903423-5

Inspirational Insights Counselling, Inc.
Red Deer, Alberta Canada
www.inspirationalinsightscounselling.com

Dedication

Dedicated to all those who read this book and seriously search find themselves.

How to Use the Books

Each book is set up in sixty short thoughts that can be used as a daily reflective meditation. Take the time to read what it says and think about it throughout the day. You can ask yourself the questions "How does this relate to me?" "What can I learn from it?" "What can I do differently?" and "Did that work for me or do I need to change something else?"

Book Contents

Reflective Meditations:
Understanding
My
Authentic Self
Photography and Script
By Audrey Tait, MS

Contents

Introduction

You may come to a time in life when you realize that you do not understand who you really are. This is what happened to me a number of years back. Different circumstance in my life did not allow me to understand who I was—what did I feel, what did I like, and what did I want? These are just some of the questions that I started asking myself. You may have similar questions. Come with me on a journey of self-discovery of your authentic self and discover who you really are, not the person others are trying to tell you that you are or who they think you are.

This book is set up in sixty short thoughts that can be used as daily reflective meditations. Take the time to read each thought and then think about it throughout the day. As you reflect on what the thought means to you, ask yourself "How does this relate to me?" "What can I learn from it?" "What can I do differently in my own life?" and "Did that work for me or do I need to change something else?"

Understanding Who I Am

Day 1 Looking for my authentic self

Today is a new day for me! I want to understand who I really am—my authentic self! For me, as the author, it was a question that I asked myself a number of years ago. My life had been going along, but I realized that I didn't really know who I was. "What did I like?" "What did I think?" "How did I really relate to others in social settings?" "What were my real emotions?" "What did I need?" "What did I want?" and "Who was I deep inside of my heart?" These may be questions that you have already asked yourself but have not found answers to, or perhaps they are questions that you want to consider on a deeper level. Come with me on this journey as we explore ourselves and find who we really are.

Day 2 Boundaries—What are they?

There are boundaries between me and other people. Many people may not understand this idea of boundaries. It may be new to me, or it may be something I have explored for some time. Somewhere between others and me there are boundaries—physical boundaries, social boundaries, emotional boundaries, and other forms of separation. A boundary is where I end and the other person begins.

Sometimes these boundaries are enmeshed, so we aren't sure where the boundaries really exist. When land and sea have boundary issues, as in hurricane, a lot of damage occurs. This can also happen in my life and my relationships—it is what happens when I do not learn to know who I am.

Boundaries can be the opposite of being enmeshed too—they can be very rigid. These boundaries are not flexible and cannot change in different situations. In relationships with rigid boundaries, the child is essentially prevented from changing and growing up, or a spouse is not able to change over time. This can cause numerous problems that leave a person finding other ways to cope, often in unhealthy ways.

Healthy boundaries are flexible and can change as the situation requires or demands. Boundaries are a big issue in knowing who I am. Boundary violations cause me to not know who I am.

Day 3 My authentic self and boundaries

Knowing my authentic self in relationships is not always easy. I cannot find myself through the actions of others—feeling good because of someone else's accomplishments; for example, my child cannot live my dreams for me. I also cannot allow others to define who I am or what I like; for example, being told I like green and not blue. Knowing my authentic self is what comes from within me —yes, I really do like blue and I will find and live my own dreams.

Knowing my authentic self includes recognizing the boundaries that exist between me and other people. In the days and weeks to come, the meditations in this book will help me better understand my physical self, my social self, my intellectual self, my psychological (emotional) self, my sexual self, and my spiritual self.

Understanding My Physical Self

Day 4 My body

I have a physical body regardless of my age. My body is the house that holds who I am. I did not choose my body. I did not choose how my body looks. The genes I received from my biological parents determined a lot of how my body looks and functions. The epigenetics is the expression of the genes (they can be turned on and off), what determines some of the current ways that my body functions. During this reflective moment, I will explore the part of me that is comprised of my physical self.

Day 5 Health issues

I may have health issues, such as heart disease, stroke, cancer, or diabetes or the risk of them, that are inherited from my birth parents. This I did not choose and I cannot change. What I can choose is how I live my life—and my lifestyle may improve and/or reduce my risk of developing even diseases that I am genetically predisposed to. This means my body will become healthier so that I can be healthier mentally as well as spiritually. Adopting a healthy lifestyle will mean making changes in how I live. This is a slow process, as change comes slowly. One of the best things I can do is to walk—this produces physical benefits as well as promotes emotional stability. Another area that brings significant change is eating a healthy diet. I am willing to make changes to improve my life.

Day 6 The way I look

I may or may not like the way I look. Self-acceptance is the first step in moving forward with this issue. As I decide that I am okay just as I am, I can choose to improve the way I look. I choose the clothes that I wear; I can choose ones that make me look better and that are pleasing to the eye. I choose the way I style my hair; I can choose something that is flattering. If I wear glasses, I can choose glasses that are appealing and fashionable. Then, there is the issue of body weight. If my body is not at a healthy weight, then I can choose to change this. It may take a lot of hard work. I may need help to reduce my weight, and I can choose to find safe people to help me change.

Day 7 Body and emotional connection

My body affects the way I feel. When my body is sick—if I have a cold or the flu, for example—my emotions are affected too. I do not feel on top of the world or very positive or grateful in life. This is the symbiotic relationship between the body and the mind and the soul. It also goes the other way. If I do not feel on top of the world or my emotions are down, then my body does not feel as good either. I have the power to decide to change how I think and reflect—and so I can affect my emotions. I can decide to treat my body healthily so that I am more likely to feel better. I want to make changes today, so that I can get to know myself better and to feel better—to be in my creative zone more often.

Day 8 Sexual as in the physical

Part of my physical health is my sex organs and hormones. I am male or female; those are the sex organs that I was born with. For a male it is testicles, penis, and sperm along with male hormones. For a woman it is breasts, vagina, uterus, clitoris, fallopian tubes, and eggs enough for a lifetime. Along with this comes the female hormonal cycle. This affects who I am—it affects my emotions and social interactions. In finding my physical sexual self, I choose to endorse who I am. If this is not possible, I will explore it with professional help.

Day 9 Physical health

The physical body that I have is what I was given through my genetic makeup from my birth parents. This I cannot change. But I can change the way that I treat my body. Proper exercise, nutrition, fresh air, sunlight, and water are all part of what my healthy body needs. I can learn to meet these needs—I can start making changes to become healthier. I will take responsibility for my physical health.

Day 10 Nutrition

What I eat has a lot to do with the way I feel, the way that I look, and how I reflect upon myself. Eating a balanced diet is the goal. This can be met by following the food guide for the country that I live in. Numerous diseases stem from improper nutrition. Our past illustrates this. Consider the lack of vitamin C and scurvy in the armies of years ago. Sometimes it could be the difference between life and death. Even a person who is obese can be malnourished. If I am unable to eat a healthy diet, then I must consider using a multivitamin and mineral supplement.

Day 11 Exercise

Exercise can have a profound effect on me personally. It is a great mood stabilizer. The next time you are angry, just try doing something that is physical—taking a walk, jogging, skiing, chopping wood, or something else physical—and you will see what I mean! For years, people have talked about the runner's high, the intense rush of good feelings that come with intense exercise, and this is what I am talking about too. I may not be able to run or take on extreme physical pursuits; however, with my doctor's permission I may be able to go for walks outside or just slowly walk around a mall. This is just a beginning of me taking control of my life and how I want to feel and who I want to be. I will start today!

Day 12 Changing

I did not choose my physical body or how it functions. Yet there are things that I can choose to keep it healthy—for example, what I eat, how I exercise, when I get fresh air, and how I get sunshine. I can choose to accept the way I look; if I do not like the way I look, I can choose to change it by being careful how I dress and by working toward a healthy weight.

Understanding My Social Self

Day 13 My social self

When considering my social self, there is the tug of my individual self and my social interactions with others. I need to learn how to be social with myself. With practice, I can enjoy sitting down with a hot cup of tea, taking a warm bath, or going for a walk by myself. I can be comfortable with myself and not allow the negative criticism from the past to depress me. The other part of socializing is being connected to others, which is something our brains are wired for. Connecting with others in a healthy way means having a conversation, one that does not include manipulation, control, or abuse.

Creating and respecting boundaries are important for such connections to happen. I choose to be safe.

Day 14 My goal in social settings

My goal in social settings, whether with family or friends, is to not lose "who I am." In social situations, a blending occurs between myself at my core level and the core of the other person(s). When this is done in a healthy environment, a very satisfying relationship develops and all involved are allowed to feel good about themselves. When this does not happen and the other person is manipulating, controlling, or abusive (verbal, physical, or sexual), I do not have to tolerate this. I can put boundaries around what needs to be changed. This will be a process that takes time and I may need help in establishing these boundaries.

Day 15 Socially with myself

One of the hardest things for many people to do is to be social with themselves. This means spending time alone with myself—no one to interact with; no radio, television, or Internet; and no other source of entertainment. It does not come easy. The voices in my head can keep coming and give me no peace. This is where I want to learn to slow down and allow my body to relax—deep breath from the diaphragm—and let my mind quiet down. I will need to work at this. I can choose to accept myself for who I am and not allow the voices of others to dictate "who I am." I can let go of the old tapes that say, "I am unworthy, helpless, and unlovable." Those are the tapes that keep me from knowing who I really am and do not allow me to be social with myself. I choose to ignore the old tapes and develop new ones instead: "I am worthy," "I am helpful," and "I am lovable!"

Day 16 Introvert/extrovert

In being social with others, I may be an introvert or an extrovert. This does not matter. When I learn to feel comfortable being social with myself, I will be more social in other situations as well, such as with family members, friends, and at work. This is because once I am comfortable in my own skin, I will be comfortable anywhere. I will be able to add to the discussion as I want to or choose to; it will not matter whether I am an introvert or an extrovert.

Day 17 My social self in family

Spending time around family and being social with family members can be difficult. There is a history that runs for many years or even decades. If abusive conversations have occurred in the past that have not been resolved, then these relationships may not always be a safe place to be. When there is manipulation and control, whether overt or covert, it's important to set boundaries around what I am willing to hear or see. Certainly, if physical or sexual abuse has occurred in the relationship, then I need to set firm boundaries around this. Even if I have "let go" or "forgiven" those involved, it is still critical to set healthy boundaries. Letting go or forgiving another does not mean I must trust that abuse will not happen again. There should always be boundaries in place to protect myself and others—especially young children—around these issues. It lets me heal and really learn who is my authentic self.

Day 18 My social self with friends

Being social around friends is a little different from being with family. I get to choose who I want to have as friends. While

I still need to have boundaries in place to protect myself from manipulation, control, and abuse, it is easier to decide to simply not spend time around these types of people. In friendships, I can learn to choose friends so that there is give-and-take in the relationship. If one gives more than the other, then this is an unbalanced relationship. I choose to have friends who are equal to me.

Day 19 My social self at work

Being social around friends at work is different from being social with my friends. There are fewer people to choose from. The level of my commitment to them will usually be more of a casual relationship. If I become overly involved, it may negatively affect my relationships at work and my job performance. This is an area of relationships to be careful about; it may need some extra thought on my part.

Day 20 My social self at parties

Being social at parties produces its own challenges, especially if alcohol or other drugs are being used. Being social in party settings may be easier for some if they have had something to drink. The boundary here is not having so much that you cannot look after yourself—making sure that nothing has been added to your drink, making sure that you do not end up doing something that you will regret later, making sure that you get home safely, which includes having a designated driver. If you cannot live by these boundaries and your own boundaries, then it is time to seek help from a professional today. These may not be your issues, as you do not go to parties with alcohol and drugs; that is excellent for you. Still, you need to have boundaries around how you socialize at parties.

Day 21 Social relations

In order to find my authentic self in social relationships, I first need to be able to spend time alone with myself and be comfortable with it. Then, I will be more likely to feel comfortable in social settings—to be able to talk and communicate at my choosing or to be able to just listen to what is going on around me. It will also be easier to set my boundaries and not tolerate behavior(s) that puts me down and makes me feel uncomfortable. I choose to learn to be by myself and be comfortable with it.

Understanding My Intellectual Self

Day 22 My intelligence

My intelligence is something that I may not have full control over. Some of it is governed by the environment where I grew up and some by the genes that I received from my birth parents. Then, there may be health setbacks along the way that can affect my intelligence. A brain injury or meningitis or drugs are just some of the issues that can affect my intelligence. Regardless of what has affected my intelligence in the past, it is my responsibility to choose how to use my brainpower. I can choose either to stimulate my intelligence in healthy ways or to do things that will decrease it.

Day 23 Drugs affecting my intelligence

Some drugs (prescription and non-prescription) may affect my thinking and intelligence. Perhaps I was given such a drug as a baby or child and I had no choice in the matter. Or maybe I needed to take a drug like this due to a medical condition. Or it could simply be that I took drugs as a way to deal with my feelings and to escape what was happening in my life. Now, I have to deal with the matter as best I can. I can find the right support people, develop healthy boundaries, and choose to live to the best of my ability, incorporating as much serenity and peace into my life as possible.

Day 24 Fetal alcohol syndrome

One type of drug injury to the brain that is preventable is fetal alcohol syndrome—that is, injury that occurs when alcohol in the mother's body crosses the placenta into the unborn child and affects the brain. Depending on what time in the pregnancy alcohol exposure occurs, different area(s) of the brain may be affected. Women should avoid alcohol when they are pregnant as well as when they are thinking about getting pregnant. Also, men can help by supporting their female partners by not drinking during this time.

Day 25 Brain injury affecting my intelligence

At any time during life—from infancy to the present day—I could have an accident that results in a brain injury. Such injuries may occur while enjoying something simple in life, while riding in a car, or during a mishap on the job. The consequences of a brain injury vary depending on exactly what happened and what area(s) of the brain were affected. If I have suffered a brain injury, I have choices to make. I choose to find the right support people, set healthy boundaries, and live life to the best of my ability with as much peace and serenity as possible.

Day 26 Cognate

Cognate is the way that I do things; this is different from personality. Cognate is static and does not change over time. When I determine how I do things, it helps me to be proactive in planning to do other things. For me, as the author, I am good at assessing things—taking the good out of what has been done and adding what is necessary.

When I know how I do things, I am more comfortable and I do not have to take so much thought to carry out the process. So, when I am doing something new, I can plan to take more time to think about it as I know it may not be so comfortable at first. I will start to notice how I do things.

Day 27 What makes me?

Although my intelligence is part of what makes me who I am, my job does not determine who I am. My job is what I do to earn a living, to pay the bills and have a place to live, to buy food to eat, and to have clothes to wear. (This is especially needed in the northern climates where it is cold in winter with snow on the ground.) I use my intellect on the job. It is what makes me different from my colleagues—my ideas, my opinions, and my way of doing things. In being myself on the job, I can express my ideas and opinions when the opportunity arises and keep them to myself when it is best to do so. This is a boundary that helps to keep me safe on the job.

Day 28 My brain wiring

The brain is wired with many different connections that help me from day to day.

For example, these connections allow me to avoid the need to make many simple, recurring decisions, such as which route to take to work. I can drive to my workplace practically on autopilot. Then, when I want to go another way, my brain still has me going the same way. That is where I need to concentrate more to get to the right place. The awesome thing about connections in the brain is that the brain has the power to make new ones. This means that with time and effort, new connections form that help me meet new challenges, like overcoming drug addictions and bad habits. (The old wiring does not disappear, so one can still go back to the old habit if they are not careful.) Research is showing that even people who have had a stroke can form new connections that allow them to move their arms and legs again. Amazing!

Day 29 Growing older

Growing older is an inevitable part of life. Part of aging often includes a mental decline. This can be slowed by stimulating the mind; for example, by learning to sing or play a new piece of music, putting together jigsaw puzzles, or doing sudoku and other challenging mental activities. Some people stay active by working past retirement age, others do volunteer work, and still others get involved in family relations and in the lives of their grandchildren.

Day 30 Protecting my intelligence

My intelligence is precious and needs to be protected. There are many ways that it can be affected, including exposure to drugs and accidents to name just a few. To avoid the decline that comes with years, it is wise to stimulate the brain. To keep my mind clear, I choose to keep it healthy, well, and stimulated.

Understanding My Psychological (Emotional) Self

Day 31 My emotional self

Depending on the environment that I grew up in, I may have very stable emotions (serenity, peace, happiness, and hope). Or I may be either very numb in my emotions or overactive with my emotions. Then there are those who are so numb from trauma that they may be unable to feel or name their emotions. Also, there are the people whose emotions are over the roof and seem unable to calm down at times. Where are my emotions most of the time?

Day 32 Anger

Anger is what I feel when someone has broken my boundaries. It may be something simple like not doing as I asked or walking into my space without my permission. It may be more complex like a legal issue that I have to deal with. And it can be anything in between. Controlling, manipulative, and passive-aggressive behaviors are all types of boundary crossing or violations. They make me angry. This is where I get to choose how I want to handle the situation. I can scream at others, which only makes the situation worse. I can internalize the situation and become anxious and/or depressed. Or I can learn to be calm and assertive and state what I need. This may not be easy depending on the other person.

Day 33 Guilt

Guilt takes many forms. There is the good kind of guilt that tells me I did something wrong. This is something that can be fixed and turned around, and life will go on. It is not a lasting feeling. Then there is the false guilt. This is the guilt that makes me feel worthless, as if I cannot do anything right. This is what I feel when others manipulate and control me. An abused child feels such guilt after enduring abuse, especially physical or sexual abuse. No one should have to feel this type of guilt. Fault never lies with the victim of abuse, especially a child. This guilt needs to be changed! If it is something that I feel, I will start to eradicate it by telling myself, "I am not guilty of what he/she did to me."

Day 34 Shame

Shame is a difficult emotion that goes very deep. It says "I am bad." The feeling of shame goes right to my core. Guilt is something that will pass and can be eliminated by correcting the problem. Shame that says "I am bad" also says "I am worthless." It takes a long time to change the negative tapes that are involved with shame. I can start by saying, "I am worthwhile," "I have value," or "I am special." I will begin today.

Day 35 Sadness

Sadness comes up after one realizes that life did not have to be so negative, so full of guilt, or so full of shame. That is another way of saying, "I could have healed before now and life could have been different." It is normal to let feelings of sadness arise, to feel the tears well up in the eyes and run down the cheeks. Let this happen. It soon will turn to a different emotion. The more this happens, the more there is room for happiness, peace, serenity, and gratitude.

Day 36 Happiness

Happiness is a feeling that everyone seems to be striving for these days. Yet, many seek happiness in the wrong places. Money cannot buy happiness; a mansion or big house will not make one's heart sing; and relationships cannot provide a long-lasting sense of delight. Rather, happiness is something that I need to find within. It is a commitment in life; it comes through living an intentional life! It develops when I am intentional about how I react to the circumstances around me—or, more likely, how I choose not to react to the negative going on around me. I want to take control of what I can control and not react to what I cannot control. This will bring happiness.

Day 37 Peace

Peace is the calm after the storm—when I can sit and take in the essence around me and just feel the environment. This comes from the core of the body with deep breathing and the feeling that "I am okay." For me, as the author, it comes with lots of "Mmmmmmms . . ." with the release of the breath. Try it—you will like it. What a sense of being! It is something that I want to feel often.

Day 38 Serenity

As I change my life, peace and serenity become more and more what I feel. I will experience more and more snippets of time with serenity until my life is completely lived in serenity. This does not mean that I will not have to make requests for people to change their behavior around me or that I will not need to be assertive at times or set boundaries. I do not need to be a doormat for someone else. Living with serenity means that I can take action and be assertive when necessary and not lose my serenity over it. This is a skill that takes time to learn.

Day 39 Gratitude

Gratitude has a lot to do with my outlook in life. It is easy to go through life thinking about all the negative things that happen to me. It is something else to go through life thinking about the positive things in life.

Focusing on the positive things in life can be a life-changing experience. It will not always be easy to cultivate this habit, to find the positive or gratitude in a negative circumstance. Yet it certainly will bring more happiness, peace, and serenity. It will also bring a different atmosphere around me —something that others will likely notice over time and will probably like very much. I will be positive in my life.

The idea is to be able to live a life with an abundance of peace and quiet, where emotions do not become so overwhelming or so numb that one cannot feel them.

Understanding My Sexual Self

Day 40 Sexuality

Sexuality is a hot topic in our society. You may have come from a family that did not talk about sex, a family where everything was sexualized, or a family where sex was healthy and could be talked about freely. Regardless of my past or my age, I am a sexual being. It was part of my genetic code when I was born. To deny my sexuality is to deny a part of my innermost being. There is a relationship between sexuality and spirituality (discussed in the next section). As one aspect of the self grows so does the other; to deny one is to deny the other. Religion that stifles sex also stifles spirituality. Those are hard words to contemplate for some. What am I going to do about this?

Day 41 Normal sex

In our society, sex between a husband and wife has been the norm for many years. Today, that is changing. We live in a very sexualized society. For some belief systems, this makes it very hard to stay committed—one man and one woman with no sexual relationships outside of marriage. This is a choice that I have to make for myself. For others, whether married or not, sex is permissible anytime; this is another choice that a person has to make. I will make sexual choices that are best for me within my belief system.

Day 42 Sexual identity

My sexual identity was predetermined from the time when I was growing in the womb. This is something I did not have a choice about and neither did my birth parents. I can learn to be content with my sexual identity; it may be the best thing for me. Yet, in our society we have choices if we do not feel comfortable in our own skin. This is not an easy decision to make and needs to be assessed with the help of a professional. For the rest of us, we can choose to support people who have views different from our own. For some groups of people, this may be extremely hard to do—it is a choice to seriously consider. Certainly, treating all of humankind with respect is essential.

Day 43 Sexual abuse

My sexuality may be something that has been violated by another person. I may have been sexually abused as a child or sexually assaulted (raped) as a teen or an adult. Sexual abuse or sexual assault does not make me who I am. It is a violation of my body, a violation of my self, a violation of my sexuality, and a boundary violation. It is a violation that is at the heart of me. It was not my fault. I did not cause it and I am not guilty of it. Again, I will say, "IT IS NOT MY FAULT!" I do not have to keep it a secret if it happened to me. I do not have to protect the guilt of the perpetrator. I can seek help! I can break the news. I can choose to seek help from a trusted friend—someone who will help me through the process—a counselor, a protection agency if I am young, a teacher, or the police. I will get help today.

Day 44 Hypersexuality or sexual addiction

For some, especially those who have been sexually abused or assaulted, sex became an addiction—it has a compulsive component to it and the person needs more of it to get the same effect. This is a serious matter and requires intervention, especially if it gets out of control. Stopping the denial of this issue is important and seeking treatment is essential. Do not delay today if this is an issue for you! Go on the Internet and look up help for sexual addiction. If you are in a partnership with someone who has this problem, you also need help—seek it today. Go to www.sexhelp.com

Day 45 Sexual anorexia

There may be a reason I do not like sex and that I avoid it even within a legal marriage. This is called sexual anorexia. Although there is no normal number of times per week to have sex, some used to think three times a week was standard but even that has changed with our fast-paced society. Something is not right if I do not like sex at all, never enjoy having sex, and avoid sex at all costs. This is defined as sexual anorexia and it is not normal. It would be best to seek the help of a sex therapist to determine what the issue is so that it can be treated. I might also need the help of a physician to find out if I have a medical concern that may make sex uncomfortable. If this is an issue for me, I choose to seek professional help today.

Day 46 Sexual diseases

Sexual diseases should not be ignored. HPV and HIV are two diseases that can destroy a person's health and end in death. Then there are other diseases that can also be contracted and passed from partner to partner. If I have been sexually active and think that I may have contracted a sexually transmitted disease, I will get it checked out and be tested. Although this is not a pleasant thing to do, especially for people who have been sexually abused or sexually assaulted, it is critical. I will tell my emotions, "I do not want to do this, but it is essential." I will do it. It could literally save my life.

Day 47 Sexual activity

Regardless of my sexual past, to know myself sexually is to explore what I like, what turns me on, what turns me off, what I am comfortable with, and what I do not like.

This may take a while for me to learn. It may start with simple things like having a hot bath with quiet music, soft lighting, candles, and relaxing scents. This could lead to trying different stimulations in a sexual relationship. The goal is to find what I like, not what someone else may think I like. This is where I get to decide my personal preferences. It is also where I get to say, "No, I do not like that" or "Yes, I do like that." This is me at one of my deepest levels; it is also me at a deep spiritual level.

Day 48 Sexual boundaries

Sexuality is a significant part of who I am. It may be something that I have denied; it may be something that I have expressed in unhealthy ways; or it may be something that I have a healthy relationship with. Perhaps others have broken my sexual boundaries, causing me sexual and emotional harm. Or maybe others just do not understand me sexually and put me down for my choices. Today is a new beginning; I will choose my sexual boundaries in all areas of my life.

Understanding My Spiritual Self

Day 49 Spirituality

Spirituality is finding that deeper purpose in life. "Why am I here?" "What is my purpose?" "What can I do to leave this earth a better place?" "What is my legacy?" and "How can I help others?" These are questions that one asks at some time in life. Some people ask them earlier in life and others later. Have you thought about these kinds of questions? Know that it takes time to answer questions about spirituality; they are not issues that can be determined in a couple of minutes. I will start to think about these questions over the next number of days and weeks.

Day 50 Healing

When faced with a crisis or when trying to flee from the hurt of the past, it is difficult to do forward thinking or to contemplate one's purpose and how to give back to society. Being overreactive in life (rage, fight, or flight) or low in energy (submit, feign death, or recuperation) makes finding purpose all the more difficult. Healing the trauma and hurt is the first order of recovery and forward movement. This is walking through the pain to find the gratitude on the other side. It may be a strange concept that there is always reason to be thankful, even in times of great difficulty. This is a lesson that I am still learning and will be for a long time. The next time something negative happens to you, look for the positive part of it. Find something that you can be thankful for and say, "Thank you" out loud. I can learn to be positive.

Day 51 After healing

After healing, it is possible to start to think of my legacy—how do I want to help other people and what do I want to leave behind for others to remember me by? When thinking about this, it is good to think about what I am good at, not in order to puff myself up because I am better than others or to think that I must give and give and give to the point of not taking care of myself. Rather, focusing on my strengths will help me determine what I can do that can be of benefit to others. I have natural abilities and I have cultivated talents—how can I use them to benefit others? Perhaps my best gift is something as simple as my smile, and yet smiling can help change the brain neurochemistry of others. What is it that you can do to help others?

Day 52 Religion versus spirituality

Religion is different from spirituality. Religion is a set of beliefs. Religion is a system of beliefs that I can choose to follow. It may be a system that I grew up with, and it may or may not be something that I follow in my present life. It may be a system that was abusive for me and that has hurt me tremendously. Religion does not make me "who I am." Religious abuse does not determine who I am deep inside. If this has been my experience, seeking healing is a part of finding "who I am deep inside of me."

Day 53 Higher Power—What are my thoughts?

Spirituality for me may or may not include "God" or a "Higher Power," as in the traditions of many support groups. This may be a concept that I have no idea about. It may be a side effect like medication that I need to tolerate in order to find support. It may be something that I do not believe in; it may be something that I have explored; or it may be something that I have a lot of experience with. Regardless, it is an issue that needs to be addressed at some point in life (perhaps later). It will take some time to seriously consider this issue. It is a part of discovering my authentic spiritual self. I choose to find out what my spiritual authentic self is.

Day 54 Spirituality and sexuality

Part of my spirituality is my sexuality. They grow together. Some religious groups restrict sexuality—they do not feel comfortable talking about sexuality or have even covered up sexual abuse. These are unhealthy practices and the people involved need healing. If you have been sexually abused by an authority figure in a church, you need to seek healing. You do not need to suffer alone. Find a safe person to talk to—again, you do not need to suffer alone. If needed, I will seek help.

The other part of spirituality and sexuality is finding the balance between my beliefs and my own sexuality. Which will set the limits of what I do sexually? I have choices to make!

Day 55 Love

True love is something to be treasured. The first love that I need to develop is love for myself—another way of saying that I can be comfortable in complete solitude. This is a healthy love, one of caring for myself. Once I have self-love, then I can reach out to others to love them and not expect anything in return. This is different from codependent love—loving others so that they might love me back. Codependent love is not healthy, as it comes from a place where I deny my own needs and wants. Another form of unhealthy love comes from a place of always wanting others to do for me what I can do for myself—being overdependent. I choose to love myself from a healthy place.

Day 56 Hope

Hope is a part of my spirituality. Hope comes with a confidence that things will work out for me in the future. Fear is the opposite of hope—taking away the knowing that my next moment and tomorrow can be a better time for me. My positive thinking will make hope more realistic. I have choices about what I want to listen to in my mind and how I react to it. Taking the time to look at all of the perspectives helps with this. Yesterday, as the author, I was tired of writing and needed a change. After a number of hours, I said to myself, "I do not need to feel like this!" It changed my attitude and reflection. I had a great evening. I choose to change my thinking into something positive—to find hope and to find gratitude.

Day 57 Serenity

At the end of the day, in finding my spirituality I also find peace in my life. If I give to others, I want to give from a healthy place—not because I have to. I am comfortable with myself, allowing me to give when I choose and am able. This will leave me with a calm serenity in my life that nobody can take away from me. This is the ultimate goal in life: peace, serenity, happiness, love, and hope. Money cannot buy any of this and money cannot take it away. Even in the worst circumstance, nothing can take this from me. It is what I will strive for in my lifetime!

Understanding Who I Choose to Be (My Potential)

Day 58 Understanding my authentic self

Understanding myself is knowing who I am: "What is it that I like?" "What are my emotions?" "What are my thoughts?" "What are my actions?" "What is my body like?" "What is my sexuality?" "What am I like socially?" and "What is my spirituality?" These are questions that we have explored in this book, and they are questions for me to continue to think about for the days and weeks to come. As the author, I still think about these questions on a regular basis. Today, while getting my hair cut it was simple decisions to make: "How long did I want my hair?" "How did I want the ends to be cut?" and "How did I want the layers to look?" These were all my decisions; I was not trying to have my hair look a particular way to please someone else.

Day 59 Healing

As my healing comes from the trauma of the past, it is easier to find myself—"To get to know who I am," "What I like," "My authentic self." As the healing comes, I am able to start looking at my purpose in life—what I want to leave as a legacy. The last fifty-eight days of reflective meditations have been just the start of really understanding myself. It is the work of a lifetime. Boundaries are meant to be flexible and change with time. Today, I may be willing to do something; tomorrow I may not be willing to do the same thing. This is healthy. I can and will choose what is best for me. Then I will choose what is best for others around me.

Day 60 Where to from here

Where to from here depends on me—what area of self-improvement do I need to spend the most time on, based on what I have learned in the last sixty days of reflective meditations? The choices are endless and I will need to choose—to be intentional. That is what life should be; living intentionally gets me to my goal(s), which comes from my purpose and long-term plans.

Thank you for coming on this journey with me. It has been my pleasure. Look for more ebooks in this series in the days to come. I wish you all the best in your journey of finding your authentic self!

Cheers to you!

Reflective Meditations
Believing in Myself
Photography and Script
By Audrey Tait, MS

Contents

Introduction

Believing in myself is something that is not always easy. There are two influences that affect whether I believe in myself—the influence that comes from others and the influence from my own internal being. When everyone else does not like or believe in what I am doing, then I have a choice: I can either listen to what they have to say and simply believe it or listen to their words through a filter that helps me look at the big picture to determine what I believe. In the past, people may have said negative things or exerted a negative influence on me so that I did not follow my dreams. These words and actions may have become the negative tapes in my head—the negative thoughts that keep me stuck and prevent me from moving forward. Believing in myself, even when no one else does, is truly living an intentional life.

Learning to Believe in Myself

Day 1 Meaning of believing in myself

Believing in oneself means that I have the confidence that I am able and capable to accomplish my intentions. For example, when I play a musical instrument within a group of people, I need to have the confidence in myself that I will play the right notes at the right time. Learning to play an instrument is a process—it takes time. Also, what I have the confidence to do on one day, I may not have the confidence to do on another day. And when I reach a different time in life, I may have the confidence to do something really difficult. There may be times when I play a solo and I really need to be sure that I know what I am doing—more self-confidence, more belief in myself is required. In reality, life is like living a "solo" because we are all unique individuals.

Day 2 My path of believing in myself

Somewhere along the path in our lives, from conception through babyhood, childhood, adolescence, and adulthood, we learn lessons about not believing in ourselves. We may allow what others say about us, along with our own internal thoughts, to take control of our beliefs and we learn not to believe in ourselves. It may be that I do not believe in myself at all, or it may be that there are some areas in my life where I doubt myself. Or perhaps I really do believe in myself when it comes to certain areas of my life, or perhaps I am slowly learning to believe in myself or already do believe in myself. Where am I on this continuum?

Day 3 My words that limit or empower me

The words you use have the power to either limit or empower you. Consider whether you use any of the following words: "I won't," "I can't," "I do not know how," "I wish I could," "I want to," "I think I might," "I might," "I think I can," "I can," or "I am." Are you using words that allow you to believe in yourself, or are you using words that limit your ability to believe in yourself? Come with me on this journey as we grow and lean into believing more and more in ourselves as we gain the confidence to truly be ourselves. To be ourselves from the core of our being—who we were really meant to be!

What Is Believing in Myself?

Day 4 Believing in myself

Believing in myself means trusting that I have the potential, capability, and ability to do something myself. It even goes beyond this—it is believing in myself even when nobody else does. It is like the bird that did not fly away when all the others did (The picture to this is in I am Wonderfully Me: Positive Affirmations for Me! *volume 1). It is knowing and believing beyond a shadow of a doubt that I can do what others think I cannot do. This is not about being arrogant or thinking beyond what is reasonable (for example, I will never be able to fly like a bird—I have the wrong body shape and weight for that). Knowing what I can do is based on past experience and having confidence that I can learn what is needed to change and follow through to reach my goals. This means believing that my brain can change and I can change.*

Day 5 Example of believing in myself

When I decided to backpack to the bottom of the Grand Canyon in 2010, I knew I could do it for a number of reasons: First, I was physically fit from following a regular exercise program. Second, I had backpacked many times in the past. And, third, I spent time preparing for the trip. There were many other factors involved as well. When others told me that I could not do it, I was not daunted by their concerns. although I did listen to them. I had a clear-cut plan and I believed in my abilities. Anything that humans are capable of, we can learn to do and we can do it well.

Day 6 Believing in myself means knowing myself

Believing in myself means knowing who I am. If I really want to believe in myself, then I need to know myself. Turning back to my adventure through the Grand Canyon, I knew the essential parts of me that I would need for the trip—the physical endurance, mental stamina, and preparation for the journey. Just as a person might examine the foundation of a house before buying it, I need to know the foundation of myself—where I have come from and where I am currently at. Then I am able to go on and make decisions that I can stand firm on and not be influenced by others who may not believe in who I am. I can also change my foundation one choice at a time to build a better foundation for the future.

Day 7 Mirror neurons affect believing in myself

Science is learning that we have mirror neurons. This means that when we are around others, we pick up on and sense what is happening with them. Therapists, for example, may sense what their client is feeling—which allows the therapist to help the client better understand what is happening. But anyone can experience the effect of mirror neurons. When we are around others, we sense what is happening to them and they sense what is happening to us—often at the subconscious level. It is important to know that mirror neurons may produce positive or negative effects. For example, when we spend time around people who are negative, we pick up that negativity ourselves. We may not even recognize the negativity but still subconsciously pick it up. This has huge ramifications. It speaks to the idea that we need to choose who we surround ourselves with and what we listen to wisely.

Day 8 Believing in myself means having boundaries

Another part of believing in myself means having boundaries. Everything in life has boundaries. Gravity is a kind of boundary; if I decide to jump, then I will land back on the earth and not float away through the sky. There are emotional, physical, mental, social, sexual, and spiritual boundaries in life. Part of knowing myself is knowing where my boundaries are in all parts of my life. If I do not know my boundaries, then I can intentionally learn where they are. From this recognition, then I can be intentional about my boundaries; if they need to change them, I can change them.

Day 9 Believing in myself means being positive

Believing in myself means being positive. This is being positive in all areas of life—emotional, physical, mental, social, and sexual. If I constantly think about the negative, then I do not believe in myself because I am not finding the hope that exists in every situation. Also, I am not allowing space for the peace, love, joy, and happiness in my life that is so crucial in helping me know and understand myself. Knowing and believing in myself means finding the positive in everything (this is not always easy to do, yet it helps the brain to change). Focusing on the positive enables me to follow through with what I believe.

Day 10 Believing in myself means loving myself

Believing in myself also means loving myself. If I hate myself, always condemning who I am, hurting myself, allow others to hurt me or abuse me in any form, then I do not believe in myself. A healthy self-love is critical to believing in myself. A healthy self-love includes looking after my own needs (emotional, physical, mental, social, and sexual). If I cannot take care of all of these needs, then I can ask for help. The person whom I ask for help has the right to say "yes" or "no," and I have the right to ask someone else if this person says "no." Another part of loving myself means being positive in my own self-talk. Saying negative things about myself is not believing in myself. Loving myself also means learning to sit by myself and enjoy the peace and quiet that comes with this.

Day 11 Believing in myself means having gratitude for myself

After I become able to love myself, I will develop gratitude for myself. After backpacking the Grand Canyon, for example, I had gratitude for having had the experience of the trip, for the physical challenge I was able to meet, for the pleasure of the pictures that I took, and for the joy of being able to share those pictures with others. With this gratitude comes a deep inner satisfaction for a job well done. It is another positive step in appreciating myself. When I reflect on the experience, I allow the deep feelings of satisfaction to rise from my core—the trunk of my body along with the long, deep breaths of inhalation and exhalation.

Day 12 Believing in myself is a journey

Believing in myself is a journey; it started with my conception and continued through my birth, babyhood, childhood, adolescence, and on to my adulthood. I am somewhere on this journey. I may not yet believe in myself for who I really am on the inside, I may not believe in myself as I want to be, or I may believe in myself to the point of believing in myself too much (have an overinflated view of myself). Learning to believe in who I really am—my authentic self—is the best journey to take from here. I will believe in my authentic self.

My Unhealthy Beliefs about Myself

Day 13 What are my unhealthy beliefs?

We become what we surround ourselves with. If our choice is alcohol and drugs, then people who drink and use are the kind of people we will associate with. If we choose to be a successful businessperson, then it is wise to find like-minded people to hang around. If I hold negative beliefs about myself, that stems from others' influence, my environment, and my own negative self-talk that is not healthy for me. Although we cannot avoid all negative people, especially family members, if the relationship is taking away from us, we need to set healthy boundaries. These boundaries determine what behavior we will tolerate and how much time we will spend around such people. What we fill our minds with is who we will become. In the past, I may not have been intentional about what I allowed into my mind, body, and soul. Now is the time to start making different choices!

Day 14 Unhealthy beliefs from others

Many of my unhealthy beliefs come from others—some from my caregivers, some from family, some from friends, some from work colleagues, and others from my own thinking. These negative thoughts say, "You cannot do that," "You do not know how to do that," "You will never succeed doing that," "Are you crazy?" and "What do you think you are doing?" So, the list goes on and on. When these kinds of negative sayings enter our brains, they gel in our minds and keep us stuck—they prevent us from moving forward. What unhealthy beliefs do I have?

Day 15 Unhealthy messages from the unconscious

Remember the mirror neurons we discussed earlier? These are the neurons that allow us to pick up ideas and images from those around us without us even knowing it. This can be a negative influence. And the negative messages do not even have to come from people we know. Having the radio and television on all the time, for example, can implant ideas into our subconscious that will have a negative impact on our beliefs about ourselves. This can affect our lives in unhealthy ways. What can I do today to make my environment more conducive to peace and serenity?

Day 16 My own unhealthy beliefs about myself

Somewhere within myself I perpetuate my own unhealthy thinking, called "stinking thinking." I continue to allow myself to remember and expand the negative thoughts from others and the environment. Doing this allows these thoughts to become more intense or to make me feel numb, taking over large amounts of my time and my energy. I have not put boundaries around this thinking. I still do not believe in myself, what I am truly capable of, and what I could do if I gave myself permission to try. I am not using positive affirmations about myself. Allowing my unhealthy thinking to continue only leads to more negative self-talk. It's time to put an end to this stinking thinking and focus on positive things, so I can develop a different perspective in life.

Day 17 The belief that I am helpless

There are three basic core beliefs that one may have; the first one is "I am helpless." Well, this is true of a newborn baby. But as the baby grows and changes, it develops physically and becomes capable of doing more and more each day. Walking, talking, and changing are just some of what the child learns. I am not speaking the truth when I say that I am helpless—I am capable of many things. If you are reading this, then you are capable of learning from reading and you can make changes as you learn. Believing in yourself is one of the changes that you can make. I can start by repeating this affirmation to myself: "I am helpful."

Day 18 The belief that I am worthless

The second core belief that one may have is "I am worthless." Being worthless means having no meaning—having no purpose, no future, and no hope. This belief comes from looking inward at all the negative things happening in my life. The solution can be found from looking outside of myself—looking upward (notice the sky and its color today) to really see what is going on around me. Another part of the solution comes from reaching out to help others, because helping others is actually a way to help myself. I can start by repeating this affirmation to myself: "I believe that I have value and worth."

Day 19 The belief that I am unlovable

The last of the three basic beliefs that one may have is "I am unlovable." This belief goes right to one's core, to the very heart of one's soul. In some ways it is the worst of the core beliefs. This belief allows others to hurt us the worst. Every baby is lovable and deserves to be loved. When an infant or child does not receive such love, or when an adult is rejected by a partner in a relationship, that person is left feeling unloved. When there is sexual rejection, it is even worse. These wounds take a long time to recover from. Healing begins with being gentle with yourself. Look for the love in healthy relationships and begin by using by using the affirmation "I am lovable!"

Day 20 The deception that I cannot believe in myself

From somewhere in the universe, I have been lied to and deceived—because I have been told that I cannot believe in myself. This deception has been there for a long time but it is not true. The questions for me to consider are "Will I continue to not believe in myself?" "Will I continue to believe the lies that I am worthless, helpless, and unlovable?" or "Will I choose to learn to believe in myself?"

Day 21 Belief in my purpose

My life has a purpose—a deeper meaning that can be found in my spirituality. As I grow more into believing myself, developing quietness and confidence in my life, I will be able to find the spiritual meaning in my life. There is a purpose for my life, a legacy for my life, and hope for my future. I was not designed to believe that "I am worthless," "I am helpless," and "I am unlovable." I can choose to change; I can choose to change and learn to believe in myself!

Changing My Unhealthy Beliefs about Myself

Day 22 What needs to change?

The first step in changing my unhealthy beliefs is figuring out what needs to be changed. Is it the environment around me—do I need to set boundaries about some of the place that I go to? Is it others around me who need to change—do I need to spend less time around certain people in my life? Is it my own thought patterns that are unhealthy for me—do I need to start reframing my thoughts? I can begin by saying, "I am helpful," "I am worthwhile," and "I am lovable."

Day 23 What are my unhealthy beliefs?

The core beliefs that some of us have in life are "I am helpless," "I am worthless," and/or "I am unlovable." There are other versions of these beliefs, like "I cannot do that," "I have no value," and "Nobody will love me." So, the questions I need to ask myself are "What are my limiting beliefs?" "What could I be doing differently?" and "What is keeping me from living my dreams?"

Day 24 How do my unhealthy beliefs affect me?

There are many ways that my unhealthy beliefs affect me. If I believe that I am helpless, I may be trying to get other people to do for me what I am able to do for myself. If I feel that I am worthless, then I may be trying to feel like I have more value. This may mean putting others down so that I feel better. It may mean manipulating and controlling others so that I come out feeling better than the other person. It may be that I feel unloved and so I will do anything to get the love back. I will do for you what I hope you might do for me in return. This can lead to codependence.

Day 25 Deciding to change my unhealthy beliefs

Whether or not to change is a choice that I have to make. If I do not decide to change, then my life will probably continue down the same path or the same course that I am on. Believing in myself take intention. I am worth every bit of intention that I put into making changes in my life!

Day 26 Changing my unhealthy thoughts

Change does not happen overnight—I cannot just go to bed and wake up the next morning as a new person. No, changing my thoughts takes time. I can start by developing positive affirmations—positive thoughts that are directly opposite of my unhealthy beliefs. For example, instead of telling myself, "I cannot do that," I can say, "I can do that." If I cannot think of what needs to be changed, then I can start by regularly telling myself, "I am helpful," "I am worthwhile," and "I am lovable." Start today, and change will come with time. Be patient with yourself—that is loving yourself!

Day 27 Changing my unhealthy environment

Changing an unhealthy environment may be easy or very difficult. If you need to stop going to the bar and drinking, you will need to find other enjoyable things to fill the time you previously spent in this activity. If you just say, "I will not go to the bar anymore," you will still want to go there—it is looking at the positive instead of the negative. It is better to have a cup half full then half empty, to see things from the positive instead of the negative.

If you need to change your environment at home, then you can limit who comes to visit and how much time the radio, mp3 player, movies, and television are on. You can also set boundaries around the types of behaviors that you will tolerate from others.

What are the ways that I may need to set boundaries in my life so that I can learn to better believe in myself?

Day 28 Setting boundaries around myself

Boundaries are everywhere in life: gravity, locked doors, edges of beds, my skin, and the space between people are all boundaries. I can make choices about where I will go, what I will do, who I will speak to, when I will speak, when I will go to bed, and when I will get up. Boundaries can be enmeshed with others so that you do not know where you begin and the other person start, or boundaries can be so rigid that they are unmovable and cannot change. Boundaries work best when they are flexible —able to change with time. What I will do today, I may not do tomorrow. When there is an emergency, I may help with something that I will not do two weeks from today. I need to be aware of boundaries and be willing to be flexible with them, so I can protect myself and so I can believe in myself.

Day 29 After changing, did it work or does it need more change?

So, after deciding to change and then making a change, I need to take a look and see if it was what I was looking for. I need to ask, "Did it flop?" "Do I need more practice?" "Do I need to change what I tried?" or "Do I just need more time to continue with this change?"

Day 30 Change

Somewhere deep inside myself, I have the ability to change and grow, to believe in myself for who I really am at my core, who I was really meant to be. That is a worthy goal to strive for. Remember the next question to always ask with change is "What is the next step?"

You are halfway through this journey with me; it is going to get real exciting from here!

Believing in Myself

Day 31 Believing who I am

I am made up from all the part of my life—the physical, social, mental, spiritual, sexual, and psychological (emotional) parts. They are all me! I cannot think about most of these parts and ignore just one. Whether I want to believe it or not, I am a sexual being. Ignoring my sexuality is ignoring my spirituality (my purpose in life), as they grow and change together. Believing in myself means believing in all of my parts. I want to endorse believing in all of myself—all of my parts. I want to be whole and believe in my wholeness.

Day 32 Believing in my physical/health abilities

Knowing my physical health and it limitations allows me to believe in myself, to know what I am capable of. From this, I can believe in myself, in what I can do, and where I can go from here. It is like my trip into the Grand Canyon: by knowing myself, I could believe in myself even when others did not have faith in me. I could take their negative comments and place them under my control by interpreting them into my framework for knowing myself. This allowed my brain to go forward with the planning. Also, knowing my physical limits—in this case that meant how much weight I could carry—allowed me to choose equipment that would both meet my needs for the trip and stay within my boundaries. Today, I want to believe in my physical abilities and my health by knowing my limits so that I can proceed within these boundaries.

Day 33 Believing in my social abilities

It does not matter if I am an introvert or an extrovert; I was born for social interactions. Brain neuroscience is confirming this. Even infants are social beings, and the need to be social continues for a lifetime. Believing in myself means knowing myself socially. It is being willing to understand that there are times when I will put boundaries around my social relations to keep myself safe, and there are times when I will expand my social relations even though this may feel uncomfortable for me. I will believe in my social self.

Day 34 Believing in my mental capacities

It may take some time to know what my mental capabilities really are. My true capabilities may very well be more than I expect or dream about. It may be that I have limited what I am able to do, or I may have allowed what others say to limit my capabilities by believing their views. For example, I was told years ago that I would never play in a band with my favorite instrument, but now I play with a college-level band. It took time to get to this point. I had to push the limits bit by bit over the years. Even an expert was wrong about what I could achieve! What limits do you need to push to believe in yourself?

Day 35 Believing in my spiritual abilities

There are so many definitions of spirituality. In this book, we're talking about spirituality as a way to help you find your purpose in life—your meaning. After one becomes comfortable in their own skin—they have become their own person, an individual—then the questions of deeper meaning start to come: "What am I here for?" "What is my purpose?" and "What do I want to give back to others?" In answering these questions, one takes into account "What am I good at?" and "What do I love to do?" Reflecting on these questions is another way that I believe in myself.

Day 36 Believing in my sexual abilities

The mere thought of believing in my sexual abilities is a loaded idea for some people. This may be an area that some do not want to talk about. Others are repeating the wounds that were inflicted upon them in this area. Some do not want to have sex, while others are totally out of control when it comes to sex. Believing in myself is knowing what I am capable of (learning about all aspects of sex) and choosing what is best for me within my belief system. This will be different for everyone. How does this affect me?

Day 37 Believing in my own psychology (emotions)

My psychology (my emotions) is something that can be viewed as a real problem. In some cultures, crying in not allowed and is viewed as a weakness. This is so far from the truth. Emotions are a part of who I am. If I am down in the dumps, then I need to take care of myself and not feel guilty because of what someone else says. If I am happy, I can share this with others. Believing in my emotions (they are valid) is one way to believe in myself. I need to not only believe in my emotions but to act on them if something does not feel right. I can learn to do this. If I sense that someone is lying to me, then I need to trust myself and look into the matter. It could save my life and my dependents. This is an example of believing in my intuition and my emotions.

Day 38 Believing in my potential

Believing in myself means believing in my potential. To know my potential, I need to know "Where I am at." Using the example of my music again, believing in my potential to join a higher level performing musical group starts with determining what level I am currently performing at. Once I have this information, I can believe in my potential and my ability to move on. This is not being arrogant. It is basing the future on fact. If I am not able to do what I want at this moment, I can still believe in myself and my ability to learn and grow so I can reach my goal. This is believing in myself and acting on my belief.

Day 39 Believing in myself, so I can love myself

Believing in myself allows me to learn to love myself for who I am—the uniqueness of "ME"! Nobody is like me. Even if I have a twin, we still have subtle differences. I am Me! Just as I said in my first book, I Am Wonderfully Me: Positive Affirmations for Me! *Volume 1, I truly am Wonderfully Me!*

Loving Myself

Day 40 Loving myself

Loving myself means taking the time to look after myself. This, in turn, allows me to love others from a healthy place. When traveling in an airplane, if the oxygen is lost in the cabin, you are instructed to put on your own mask before helping someone else. If you put on someone else's mask first, you are using more energy than the other person and so need more air (oxygen) than they do. It's like that with self-love too. You need to look after yourself first, even if others are dependent on you. This is not being self-centered or narcissistic. Narcissistic behavior is when you are trying to cover up your own wounds and demanding that others meet your needs. Truly, loving yourself allows you to spread love to others.

Day 41 Taking time to love myself

Taking time to love myself means resting and relaxing when needed. This may be simply taking a hot bath once in a while, spending time doing what I enjoy, spending time on my hobby(ies), going for a walk, being involved in music, reading a good book, traveling, or any other activity I like. If I have young children, I can take time for myself after they go to bed or find something enjoyable that we can all do together. If money is an issue, I can look for free things to do around me—there are many.

Day 42 Caring for myself

Caring for myself is part of loving myself. Caring for myself includes looking after my physical needs—as well as my mental needs, social needs, sexual needs, and spiritual needs. If my body is hungry and tired, I am more likely to make poor decisions. The first order of business would be to meet these needs as soon as possible. I carry small quantities of food with me in case I get hungry and need to eat. Eating small amounts, as needed, between meals work for me. What works for you in caring for yourself?

Day 43 Knowing myself

Knowing myself is knowing who I am. It means answering questions like "What am I capable of doing?" "What do I like to do?" "Who do I like to socialize with?" "What kind of background did I come from?" "What kind of work can I do to earn an income?" These and many more questions help me define "who I am." It helps me know the boundaries that are already around me. Do you know your own boundaries?

Day 44 Understanding myself

Understanding myself goes beyond knowing myself. When I know myself, then I can start to understand myself—and this answers the question of "Why do I do what I do?" This answer starts to give me purpose in life and living. Understanding myself is something that only I can really think about and decide —no one else can do it for me.

Day 45 Pampering myself

Part of loving myself is taking the time to pamper myself once in a while. First, I need to figure out what I like. What puts a real smile on my face and joy in my heart? What makes me feel good? Once I know this, then I need to find the time and schedule the time to treat myself to what feels good. I am special and I deserve every bit of pampering.

Day 46 Loving myself before giving of myself

For some people and some religions, one of the hardest concepts to grasp is loving myself first. The reality is that I cannot help or love someone else if I do not love myself. If I love others from an unhealthy place and give and give and give and deplete myself of my resources, I have accomplished nothing. In the meantime, I have given away my own soul, my energy, and my love until I have become empty and unable to give anymore. Compassion fatigue happens when the caregiver becomes worn out and can give no longer. To prevent this, it is important to look after myself first. This is true love.

Day 47 Giving from my heart

When I start loving myself and become a healthy person, then it is easier to help others. I have learned my boundaries around what I need and when I am able to give. It means that I have learned to say "no" when I cannot do something and I have learned to say "yes" when I can. This breaks the yoke of others trying to control me and manipulate me. Then I do not lose "who I am" at the core of my being.

Day 48 Growing to the next level

It will take a while to really start loving myself. This change does not happen overnight, although I wish it did. Practice and slow change is what is called for. From a healthy place, then, I can move to the next level—being grateful for myself.

Having Gratitude for Myself

Day 49 Why gratitude?

It may seem incredibly difficult to have gratitude for myself, especially if this is a new concept for me. Being proud of what others do—what children do, in particular—is a natural feeling when something is done well. But why can we not feel the same way about ourselves? This is not about being narcissistic or self-centered. This is about being honest about what I have done. It means taking the time to really savor success. It is not just about the reward; it is about the feeling of it at the core of my being—being able to sit and feel that gratitude!

Day 50 Small-size gratitude (small-size rewards)

Gratitude can be about the very small things—for example, the thought that I am so glad that I got that job done and no longer need to think about it. Small amounts of gratitude come from our attitude. I can either be negative—that was a horrible job—or I can focus on the positive that it is done. Being positive helps to actually change your brain chemistry and form new neural networks that bring more peace and serenity. So, working to find even small amounts of real gratitude is the way to go—even in adverse and difficult times! Even when it is hard to do!

Day 51 Medium-size gratitude (medium-size rewards)

Medium-size gratitude is somewhere between small and large gratitude. At times, this is like rewarding the smaller incremental steps in a long process. For example, if I am trying to lose weight, this might mean rewarding myself with every five or ten pounds that I lose. I might reward myself by sitting down to relax for five minutes after a hard workout. What do you reward yourself with? What can you do in the future to reward yourself?

Day 52 Large-size gratitude (large-size rewards)

The larger types of gratitude revolve around those milestones that we achieve in life and celebrate with others—winning an award, earning a degree, completing a major project at work, celebrating a significant birthday or anniversary. Sometimes the celebration is small and other times it could be very big. Certainly, there is a need to celebrate and let the accomplishment or event soak into our own well-being—to savor the moment with deep breathing, a sense of happiness, and contentment, telling ourselves, "That was awesome!"

Day 53 Self-gratitude

Self-gratitude is the gratitude that I give to myself. It comes from within. It may be very private, something that no one else will ever know about, or it may be something that I share with others. The main idea is that I need to learn to feel comfortable with rewarding myself. Part of this is being able to look at myself in the mirror every day and be thankful for who I am. It is about the positive things that I say to myself. What positive things will you say to yourself today?

Day 54 Receiving gratitude

Being able to receive gratitude is part of having gratitude for myself. So often, it seems difficult to receive gratitude graciously. Yet, learning to do this is respectful for myself and respectful for the person giving it. Being about to say, "Thank you! That is very meaningful for me" and really mean it, is excellent. This does not mean you are being boastful. Rather, being able to graciously receive a compliment shows that you are a healthy person.

Day 55 Endorsing gratitude

Endorsing gratitude is to accept gratitude. This is not letting the negative tapes in your head say, "She did not really mean that," "I do not deserve that," "He was just being nice," or some other negative thought. This is not the way we endorse gratitude. Nor are we endorsing gratitude if we say "Thank you" but then allow the negative tapes to play. Ask yourself, "Do I accept gratitude from others with grace and really mean it?" or "Do I need to change to endorse gratitude?"

Day 56 Giving gratitude

When you have learned to give gratitude to yourself and accept it from others, then it will be a lot easier to give it to others with meaning. It will come from the heart! Also, it will become a natural part of your life—giving back to others. What a gift this is! How are you going to spread gratitude into the world and make your life full of awesomeness?

Day 57 Taking it all in

Now, you have the choice of believing in yourself, loving yourself, and having gratitude for yourself. Making this choice does not come from self-centeredness. This decision comes from a healthy place that allows you to give back to others from a healthy place, to continue to believe in yourself, and to have more love and serenity in the days and weeks to come. What are you going to do with this information? Are you going to use it? Are you going to change? What is your choice?

Conclusion

Day 58 Believing in myself

Believing in myself means endorsing all of my parts—believing in all my parts, loving all my parts, having gratitude for all my parts. It is a process that takes a lifetime; it is something that I choose to continue to change over my life!

Day 59 Believing in my care

Knowing myself includes knowing my boundaries. When I know my boundaries, then I am able to care for myself and know my potential. From this point, I can reach out to others from a healthy place and give back.

Day 60 Endorsing myself to the fullest

I have an awesome potential that I may not yet fully understand. It is something that continues to amaze me as time passes. I want to continue to believe in myself. I want to become the person I was meant to be.

Reflective Meditations
Loving Myself
Photography
and Script
By Audrey Tait, MS

Contents

Introduction

Knowing how to love myself is something that took a while for me to learn. It was not something I was ever taught. I was always on the go—there was always something else to do. There was seldom time to do what I wanted or needed to do to care for myself. It took leaving a difficult relationship for me to start finding the time to love myself and look after myself.

Loving myself means understanding that I have personal needs, determining what my personal needs are, and then finding a way to meet those needs. When I do this first, then I can love others from a healthy place. The old saying "Love your neighbor as yourself" does not mean loving others more than or less than myself. I may love others more at times, and at times I may receive more love than I give—yet there is always a balance. This book is a journey of understanding what it means to love myself and how to begin doing so. Come with me on this journey.

Loving Myself

Day 1 How do I love myself?

Loving myself takes on many forms—this means loving myself in all aspects of my life. It is treating myself with respect, including what I think about myself, what I say about myself, what I do to myself, and what I do to others. Sometimes, I may be my worst enemy and other times I might be my own very best friend. Many times, life is somewhere in between these two scenarios. Life is a journey that is ever changing—as life changes, situations change and boundaries change. Come explore and learn more about how to treat yourself with love and respect.

Day 2 Loving myself starts with me

Loving myself starts with me. It is how I live life and how I treat myself in that process. Do I respect myself? Do I show compassion to myself? Do I take care of myself? Or do I treat myself with disrespect, lack of compassion, and lack of care? Or do I always give to others without caring about myself? Do I hope that someone else will meet my needs—spoken or unspoken? Do I look for love in the wrong places? Or do I know myself enough to respect and take care of myself before reaching out to help others? Am I able to find this balance?

Day 3 Loving myself is my responsibility

It is my responsibility to care for myself, to love myself, and to respect myself. This is true unless I am not an adult (then it is my job to learn to take care of myself as I grow), unless I am elderly and not capable of taking care of all my needs (then it is my responsibility, as far as possible, to state what I need), or unless I have a challenge with some aspect of life (then it is my responsibility to do as much as I can for myself). Beyond the needs of certain groups of people, it is my job to look after myself and in the process to love myself in all aspects of my life. From this healthy point of view, then I can reach out to others and have meaningful relationships, meaningful moments in life, and meaningful adventures in life. Where are you in this journey of caring for yourself and loving yourself?

Day 4 Loving myself so as to have peace

When I am in a healthy place in my life, respecting myself, caring for myself, and able to spend time with myself, then I am in a good place and able to find peace and rest. It is from this place of peace and rest that I can go out into the world around me. It is easier from this place of peace to have good relationships, be social, explore the world, be able to give to others, and be vulnerable in a sexual setting.

Self-Love—What It Is

Day 5 Self-love includes…

My self-love starts with looking after my physical needs. This includes activities like deep breathing, drinking water, getting adequate sunshine, getting fresh air, eating nutritious foods, getting adequate sleep and exercise, and avoiding unhealthy substances. These are the needs of my body. Then there are my emotional needs—accepting my emotions for what they are and learning to control my emotions if needed; accepting my intellect, regardless of what it is; being social regardless of whether I am an introvert or an extrovert; and finding my path or my purpose in life and accepting who I am as a sexual being.

Day 6 Self-love, a balance

Self-love is looking after myself and my needs. It is learning what I like/love, what I want/what I need, and what I do not want/ what I do not need. Loving myself means learning how to state what I need and what I do not need and, in this process, being able to consider the needs of others. It is a balance of everything I do in all aspects of my life. It is me being authentic and at peace with myself and the world around me. Where are you in this process of learning to love yourself?

Self-Love—What It Is Not

Day 7 Self-love is not always giving*—part 1*

Self-love is not about loving yourself and never thinking about others, never considering the needs of others. It is like a teeter-totter. The balance is in the middle. Always loving yourself would be at one end of the teeter-totter and never loving yourself would fall at the other end. The old saying "Love your neighbor as yourself" means just that: not loving others more than yourself and not loving yourself more than others. Again, it is like the balance of a teeter-totter.

Day 8 Self-love is not always giving*—part 2*

There will be times in life when one gives more than one receives in a situation, and there will be other times where one receives more than one gives. This works well in the balance of love, provided that a relationship is equal in giving over time. When I end up in the hospital for short periods of time, I need to allow myself to be helped and my dependents to be looked after by other safe people. This is all part of the ups and downs of life.

Respecting Myself

Day 9 Respecting my thoughts

The question for today is, "Do I respect myself?" There are many ways that I may not respect myself. My thoughts are the first area to consider. Do I say negative things to myself that may or may not be true, things like "Why did I do that? That was stupid" or "That was useless"? These are the types of thoughts about myself that I can choose to change, if I desire. I can choose to say something positive in my mind. For example, I have issues with remembering people's names; however, instead of saying a negative comment to myself about it, I will say, "I am working on remembering people's names." Are there things that you can say differently to yourself?

Day 10 Respecting my thoughts—who I am

Continuing on the theme of self-respect from yesterday, let's look at the thoughts that go right to the core of who we are. These include "I am worthless," "I am helpless," and "I am unlovable." There are many versions of these thoughts. All of them hurt who I am as a person and not just my behavior. To change these thoughts and variations of them, I can start by saying to myself, "I am okay, I am lovable, I have value, I have worth, and I am helpful." This is the beginning of how I can treat myself with love and respect. What can you do today to start respecting the core of your being?

Day 11 Respecting myself in all areas of my life

There are many other ways that I need to respect myself. This includes what I do to myself whether I am by myself or around others. Treating myself with respect means treating myself kindly in all areas of my life. This include looking after my damaged self, my physical self, my intellectual self, my psychological or emotional self, my social self, my spiritual self, and my sexual self. This care and respect takes on many forms in life. It takes time. It takes being intentional. Are you willing to respect yourself?

Day 12 Understanding trauma

This is a world where things do not always go as planned. Things happen to us unexpectedly. Each person reacts in different ways. Some things may be a little trauma (Little t), like hearing someone say something that hurt me; sometimes things are a big trauma (Big T), like major accidents, earthquakes, wars, natural disasters, or sexual abuse; and then there is the chronic trauma that continues happening on a long-term basis, which can be just as bad as a Big T. Everyone reacts differently to what is going on in life; something that hurts one person may not hurt another person or may hurt them in a different way. Being aware of what is going on in my life is the first step in being able to look after my damaged/traumatized self.

Day 13 My story

Loving my damaged or traumatized self is not something that I want to think about. I was brought up in a world of secrets, where there was something to ignore and not even talk about. It was too shameful. My family history was full of secrets. My marriage also carried secrets. This pattern continued until I finally reached my breaking point and could not take it any longer. It took many people to help me through the tough times, to reinforce my value/worth, love, and helpfulness. It took a long time to accept the damage and to start looking after myself. Do you have secrets and damaged parts of yourself that you have ignored for a long time—maybe even years like me? Is it time to do something about it? Remember that healing comes in safety, and looking after yourself means finding a safe place to heal. Do you need healing and are you willing to start thinking about the process?

Day 14 The beginnings of the journey

After acknowledging my personal trauma, it took a long time to see that it was having a major effect on my life—from my emotions to my relationships to my physical body. The journey of healing was a long one and is still in progress as life continues. What past and present traumas do you need help in healing from? Can you find healing from talking with a trusted friend, or do you need more professional help as I did? As you go through acknowledging your difficulties, the process is a promise that life will get better as you move along, but it may take a while. It did for me. Another part of the journey is to learn to trust the process.

Day 15 The healing journey

Are you ready to move forward on a difficult journey? The level of difficulty depends on how you have reacted to what has happened in your life. It may be something simple or something more complex; each person's journey is different—even if you are raised in the same family. Once you have decided to move forward, you get to decide how you want to take the journey, by yourself or with safe others. Remember, healing takes time and does not happen overnight. Sometimes all that one can do is open the door a crack, only to close it and wait for another day or time to open it just another crack. Eventually, the emotions subside and the door can be fully opened and left open. During this process, remember to look after yourself; just like you need to put the air mask on in the airplane yourself before helping others, you must look after yourself first right now. Deep breathing, engaging the diaphragm, helps the process by relaxing the body system. What else do you need to help you in the healing process?

Day 16 The journey is the goal

The journey is the goal, not the end product. Life will be better in the end; however, it will continually improve as time goes on. What is it that I need to do today to make my personal world a better place for me? This is the question to ask each day. Yesterday may have been a success or a failure. Today or just this moment is all that I have. What can I do to make it better for myself? What am I willing to do? What does my energy level allow me to do? Maybe all I can do in this moment is reassure myself that I am okay. Continue on this journey as best you can. That is all that you can expect of yourself and accepting that is one way to respect the damaged goods that you may feel you are.

Day 17 There is hope

Understand that at the end of the tunnel, usually one can see daylight. At first it is just a glimmer of light/hope but as it increases, it becomes more and more until you are in full daylight. And from the mess of life and the healing it brings our greatest strength emerges. Some of our most productive ideas and results come into being. Difficulties/ trauma are a training ground for our future. For me, I became a therapist and found my ability for photography and writing. What will you learn through this journey? Will it help you find more meaning and purpose in life as it did for me?

Loving My Physical Self

Day 18 Looking after my body

Loving my physical self is loving my physical body. Loving my physical body means accepting it—the way it is. I was born with the genetic code that I have. There are many things that I cannot change about the way I look, such as the color of my skin, the color of my eyes, and many other attributes. These unchangeable things I need to accept just the way they are. It may be hard for me or it may not be hard for me. There are other things about my physical body that I can alter with a lifestyle change or other help. These things I can decide to change, make an effort to change, and maintain the change over time.

Day 19 Looking after my body

Loving my physical self means looking after my physical body that I have had since birth. It is not a perfect body because I do not live in a perfect world. However, it is the best that I have, the only body that I will ever have, so taking care of it is important. This will take on many different forms and will be different for each person.

Day 20 Providing physical needs

Taking care of my body means looking after my physical needs. Breathing in air is the most important need; without it one dies very quickly. Other critical needs are pure water and nutritional food. Beyond this we can improve the body with proper rest, exercise, staying away from harmful substances, abstaining from or restricting alcohol use, and having a spirituality or trust in a Higher Power. These changes take time and are different for everyone. Starting an exercise program at an older age means seeing a physician first to make sure it is safe to start exercising. Part of taking care of my physical body is knowing what is best for me personally. What is best for me may not be best for someone else.

Day 21 Safety from self-harm

Part of the process of taking care of my body is not harming myself; this means avoiding many forms of self-harm from cutting to slapping to ingesting harmful substances (like too much alcohol, harmful drugs, unnecessary prescriptions, over-the-counter medications that are not needed, overeating, and too much of anything) to the other extreme of not providing for my body what it needs, like healthy foods, physical exercise within my ability, and whatever else is needed. This is a balance that needs attention. Part of learning how to take care of our physical body is dealing with the strong emotions that drive us to harm ourselves so we do not need to deal with our emotions.

Day 22 Physical safety

Taking care of my physical body includes making sure that I am physically safe. This is physical safety. If I am in a place where my body might be hurt physically, what do I need to do in this moment? I may not be able to escape, so what can I do to lessen the hurt and escape as soon as possible? Do I need help from others—do I need to find shelter or go to a women's shelter? Safety is important!

Day 23 Physical boundaries

Another part of loving my physical self is being aware of the physical boundaries around me. These boundaries can change with time and place and who or what the issue is. Being aware when others come too close for my comfort is part of this process. What do I need to do to keep this space around me a safe place? What do I need to be intentional about and what do I need to do should this become an issue? For me, someone who comes into my personal space makes me subconsciously want to back up. It also makes for a very uncomfortable conversation.

Day 24 Accepting my intellectual/cognitive ability

Loving my intellect starts with accepting my intellectual/my cognitive ability. My cognitive function may be low or high or somewhere in the middle. Some of this is determined by my genetic code and some of it comes from the environment that I have been in. There is the nature versus nurture debate. Wherever you are currently with this issue of cognitive development, it is your job to accept it. Have you been able to accept it?

Day 25 Some things can be changed

There are things that interrupt our cognitive function. It may be an injury, a trauma, low blood sugar, or something else. It could be the use of illegal drugs or an addiction. Sometimes, it could be something that we have no control over. If there is something that influences our intellectual ability in a negative way, it might be something that we can change—that we have a choice about—that we can be intentional about changing. Maybe it is something that can be managed. Is there anything you can do about it?

Day 26 Thinking about change

Change may take a little bit of time or may be a long-term process. Sometimes it may be difficult and persistence is what is needed. If I do not have persistence, then taking one step at a time is all that I may be able to do. For me, starting something is what gets me going. Once going, it is easier to keep moving forward. This is the same as moving an object—once it is moving, it is easier to keep it moving.

Day 27 Making changes

Cognitive function is what helps me think about change. Sometimes, even before I think about change, my mind will start thinking about the process. Then, more thinking is needed before I decide to change and then actually make the changes. From this perspective, after the changes are made, then I need to maintain the changes. Is there something that you need to begin thinking about—something that you need to change?

Day 28 Supporting my intellectual self

Life is always changing. Each new day is different. What I needed yesterday in my cognitive reasoning will be different today. It may not be something that I can plan for. Yet, there are things that I can do to help improve my cognitive ability. This goes back to self-care and looking after my body with my lifestyle—the positive thing I do to look after my body in the foods that I eat, the exercise that I get, and the water that I drink will make positive changes to improve my cognitive ability.

Day 29 Stimulating cognitive function

Life is always changing and so is my intellect as I go through life. The longer I live, the more life experiences that I have. Stimulating my brain on a regular basis is a way to keep mentally active. What do you like to do that will stimulate your brain? What do you like to learn that is new—is it traveling to a new place, is it playing music? What is it that you can intentionally do to stimulate your brain?

Loving My Psychological/Emotional Self

Day 30 Emotions

Loving myself is loving my psychological/ emotional self. This means allowing myself to have emotions, to feel my emotions, to express my emotions, and to be okay with my emotions and okay with others around me seeing my emotions (if it is safe to do so). This is a tall order. Many of us have grown up not being able to express our emotions. Some of us have stuffed emotions to the point of being numb from them and not being able to even put a name on them. Then there is the other side where people express their strong emotions (such as anger) at another person and feel relief from it themselves with no regard for those around them. Neither process of stuffing emotions or releasing them to the harm of others is good. Somewhere in the middle is the ability to balance this and respect oneself.

Day 31 Allowing myself to have emotions

When it comes to respecting my emotional self, the first place to start is with myself, to allow myself to have emotions with myself. Emotions are not right or wrong. They are simply part of me—part of who I am. It is okay to have personal emotions just like it is okay to have personal wants and desires. It is okay for me to express my personal emotions when I am alone or in a safe place. Safety is the key. One can learn to control emotions until one finds a safe place to release them, if desired. For me, it was a learning process to allow the tears to run down my face; this was true even when I was alone with myself. What part of emotions do you need to allow yourself to accept?

Day 32 Dealing with stuffed emotions

Stuffed emotions come from not dealing with what is going on in my world. When there is a broken boundary of mine, spoken or unspoken, that I have a reaction to—that does not get dealt with and is stuffed and left stuffed—then it leads to depression. Dealing with this means dealing with what is going on before it gets stuffed. It might mean learning to be assertive and clearly state my boundaries. If that does not work, it might mean planning what I do so that I am safe emotionally. It might mean staying away from a difficult event or person. It might mean having a safe person to talk to about a situation after the event so as to de-escalate what has happened. It might mean doing self-care (like deep breathing, exercise, or something else that I find relaxing) to release some of the numb feelings. What do you do to deal with emotions so they don't get stuffed?

Day 33 Dealing with strong emotions

Strong emotions are the opposite of stuffed emotions. These emotions could include stages of anger or any other strong emotion. Again, they are the results of some type of boundary violation. One of the best ways to deal with strong emotions is to do some form of exercise. I remember twice in my life when I was extremely angry. Both times, it was exercise that de-escalated the anger. Once was going for a walk for thirty minutes and the other time was going downhill skiing for about forty-five minutes. At some point in time, after the strong emotions have subsided, you may need to deal with the boundary issue that was violated. What is it that you can do to help deal with strong emotions?

Day 34 My emotions and others' emotions

As much as I need to love myself, there is the other side of the story. Others have emotions and I need to be able to allow others to have their own emotions. After I take care of my own emotions, I need to allow others to do the same. This does not mean that I allow others to treat me without respect. It means that I am willing to allow others to have emotions and be safe with it for both of us.

Day 35 Learning to be at peace in my inner world

Part of learning to deal with our emotions is being able to sit with ourselves and listen to our inner self, our inner voice. This is the ultimate goal in life—being at peace with yourself. Is this something that you find scary, hard to do, or just uncomfortable? Or is this something you have learned to do over time and are very comfortable with? For me, this has involved a process of learning. It has developed with time. Having internal peace becomes very useful in hanging out with others like family and friends. It means moments of silence are not awkward. It means I do not feel like I need to be talking all the time. It provides a measure of security in a situation. Are you willing to work toward a place where you are comfortable with yourself?

Loving My Social Self

Day 36 Loving my social self

Loving my social self means loving myself socially—this involves being social with myself, having moments of quiet time and enjoying them, being social with others, being comfortable with the ebb and flow of conversation, and not always having to be talking or listening. This is all true regardless if one is an introvert or an extrovert. For good socialization to happen, it needs to be in a safe environment. It is a give-and-take situation to look after oneself.

Day 37 Being social with myself

Being social with myself is being able to sit with myself and be at peace with myself.

This is the goal of where I want to be in life. It is a process to get there. Maybe this is not an issue for you and you are an authentic person, or maybe this is something you are still working on. Reaching this goal often involves practice. There are many different ways and times to practice this—short moments at a party, early morning before getting out of bed, in line waiting for a service, a set time of day, while exercising, going to bed, or some other convenient time. Being social with oneself develops more peace in one's life. You might like to try it.

Day 38 Being social with others

Being social with others means having a relationship. Relationships are good when there is safety around them. When others manipulate and treat one with disdain, it is not a good relationship. The other side of the coin is when I treat others with disdain and disrespect or manipulate them. Relationships need to involve an equal amount of give-and-take over time. Today, I may help you, if I am able, and tomorrow you may help me if you are available. Are your relationships healthy and balanced?

Day 39 Being an introvert

Being an introvert means that I need time alone to regenerate my soul. It means that I need time by myself to feel better. When something difficult happens to me, I want to be by myself, to think it through, to figure out what I want to do about the matter. Even if something good happens, I want time to digest it and think about it. When others want to socialize, I may want to be by myself; this is just me being an introvert. Sometimes introverts may seem like extroverts because what they do demands acting like an extrovert, yet really they are introverts. That is the way it is for me; I need time to unwind—sometimes for a few minutes and sometimes for a whole weekend —yet my job demands that I act like an extrovert.

Day 40 Being an extrovert

Being an extrovert means I need to be around other to regenerate my soul. It means I need to have others around me to feel better. When something difficult happens to me, I want to be around others. Even in the good times, I want to have others around me. I am very social—work, friends, and family are all about being social. It is a way of life for me. Even with being an extrovert, there needs to be safety in my relationships. All individuals need to contribute to the relationship without manipulation or control. This includes me and how I treat others. In the end, it needs to be an equal give-and-take over time.

Day 41 Choosing how to be social

As a part of loving my social self, I get to decide how I want to be social. Do I want to be by myself or with others? The final decision is for me to make and not for someone else to decide. If someone else makes the plans, then I get to decide if I want to be a part of the plan or not be a part of the plan. Part of that decision needs to consider my social safety. Do others allow me to be the person that I am? Are these friends that I can be authentic around? These are the friends that I want, the friends that I choose to be around.

Day 42 Spirituality…

Spirituality is a part of life regardless of what religious organization you may or may not belong to. It is about your path here on this earth. What is your purpose or your mission? And from that, what are your goals that will allow you to accomplish your purpose? Where do you see yourself in five or ten years from now? If you are young, you may have a lot of thinking to do before you are able to answer these questions. If you are middle aged, you may or may not have answered these questions; now is a good time to consider or reconsider these questions. And if you are an older person or a senior, it is never too late to start. In my mother's dying years, we talked about things that she could still look forward to with the time that had been given to her.

Day 43 My strengths

Somewhere on the journey of finding my personal path it's important to look at what I am good at doing, what I enjoy doing, and what I feel I need to do. A lot of times it is out of this that I may find my passion, and that may lead to a mission statement and the goals and path I want to pursue.

Day 44 My difficulties

I may also find what I am called to do from the desperate situations/trauma that I have been in/through. This is where our greatest strength comes from. For me, it was through enduring the tough times that led me to go back to school and get a master's degree to go along with my personal experience so that I could help others. It has become my mission to help others through therapy, writing, and speaking.

Day 45 Detours

After finding my path, there may be deviations/detours; however, the path is always there. Sometimes, I need to follow my heart until the understanding comes, giving me the reason I do something. Personally, there are times when I say or do something that just did not make total sense, yet later, I find out that for the person I said it to, it was just what they needed to hear. There are parts of life that may seem out of place, yet they were meant to be.

Day 46 Other detours

Other deviations to my path are not planned and I just need to deal with them. This could involve illness, a family emergency, accidents, natural disasters, or something else that happens and I have no control over it happening. Remember, these are just deviations and the path remains there with the personal mission and goals that led to the mission. The thing to remember is to not lose the vision. I had a health issue several years ago that had to be managed, which meant that it took longer to get things done. While my vision was still there, it has taken longer to get things done and that is okay. This is a time for self-compassion. Are there deviations in your vision /pathway right now?

Day 47 Spirituality is a journey

Spirituality is a journey that encompasses our entire life. It is never over until it is over. I can have compassion for myself for the past—how I may or may not have lived. I can appreciate what was good in the past and enjoyable, and plan for the future. I can start now with intention and choice of where I want to go and what I want to do as part of my spirituality or purpose in life.

Loving My Sexual Self

Day 48 Accepting my sexual self

My sex organs are a part of my physical self. My sexuality is a significant part of me and something that needs special attention. There are two extremes to sex, from sexual anorexia to over-sexualization/sexual addiction. Healthy sex is somewhere in the middle. Regardless, I need a healthy respect for sex and the sex organs. My job is to accept my sexuality—whatever that may look like.

Day 49 Looking after my sexual health

It is my responsibility to look after my sexual health. This takes on many different forms and will look different for everyone. It means seeing the doctor when needed. It may mean taking a break from sex for a while. It may mean asking specific questions about another person's sexual health before having sex. It may mean many different things. What does it mean for you to look after your own sexual health?

Day 50 Protecting my sexual health

There are so many things that can go wrong with sex. There are sexual diseases that can be transmitted, unwanted pregnancies that can happen. Protecting my sexual health is very important. Sometimes it may not be possible. Then it is my responsibility to make sure that I get the information afterward to continue to protect my sexual health.

Day 51 Boundaries around my sexual health

When it comes to boundaries around sex, some people have no boundaries and others have very rigid boundaries. It is helpful to have one's boundaries thought out ahead of time. It takes time and effort to decide what is right for me. Having boundaries around sex may be a new concept. Another part of having boundaries around sex is deciding places where you will not go or places where you will not be found alone with someone. Do you have any boundaries around sex? What are your boundaries around sex?

Day 52 Making changes for improved sexual health

What is it that you can do to improve your sexual health? Would losing weight make a difference? For some, weight gain or too much weight is an unconscious way to push others away sexually. Would starting an exercise program (check with your doctor first) increase your sexual enjoyment? Would working on accepting yourself increase your sexual enjoyment? For women, would strengthening your inner sexual muscles increase your enjoyment of sex? For others, taking care of your current level of sexual health is all that you need to do. How can you improve your sexual health?

Day 53 Enjoying sex

Sex was meant to be enjoyed. For this to really happen, it needs to be in a safe environment—preferably in a committed relationship. This is due to the fact that sex is as much in the brain as it is in the sex organs. Sex is also a very deep emotional part of our life. It is meant for enjoyment, so enjoy it when you can in a safe way.

Total Love for Myself

Day 54 Total self-love

Total love for myself is loving everything about me. It is accepting who I am for what I am. It is accepting all aspects of my being, from my physical and sexual self to my emotional self—total acceptance of everything. This includes the parts of me that are not the best parts of me, the parts that I want to hide from others. Total love for myself is about learning to be authentically me in all situations; learning to live at peace in my inner world; being able to spend time with myself and my thoughts and my feelings; and being at peace in the process—right down to the very core of my being. This is the ultimate aim in being comfortable in my own skin.

Day 55 Change after acceptance and self-love

From the place of total acceptance and being able to spend time alone with myself, I can look at change, if I choose. The parts of me that I can change, I can choose to change. Change is about what I can change and that is me. I cannot change another person. Trying to do so is control and manipulation. I am the only one that I can change. Yet, by changing, I can set boundaries around what others do. Others get to accept my boundaries or reject them. If others reject my boundaries, then I get to decide my next step from there. And that is as far as I can go with changing what is happening around me.

And in the End—Being Able to Love Others

Day 56 From self-love to healthy love for others

Looking after myself allows me to love others from a healthy point. The old saying "Love your neighbor as yourself" does not mean loving yourself more or always putting yourself first over others, nor does it mean loving someone else more or always putting others first over yourself. It has to be a balance. It is a delicate balance and is constantly changing with relationships, including those with family, friends, and colleagues. From the healthy state of self, it is easier to find this balance.

Day 57 Loving family

Family relationships are unique in this process. Sometimes life difficulties demand that we give more, and sometimes the difficulties mean that we accept more from others. When life has sent us such circumstances, it is important to take the time later to recover and look after ourselves as needed and time is available. When you have young children, it means finding moments to refresh yourself (this may be something that can be shared with the child that also refreshes you). It is imperative to be intentional about making time for refreshing moments.

Day 58 Loving others

It is from this healthy place of self-love or caring for myself in all aspects of my life that I can come to love others—not more than myself and not less than myself. It is a daily balance in life of loving myself, caring for family, caring for friends, and caring for colleagues. If I am sick in a hospital, I am not in a place to look after others; I need to allow others to look after me until I am healthy again.

Conclusion

Day 59 Finding the balance

This is a process of finding the balance in life to be okay with myself and reaching out to others. We were made for relationships—to have others to share our difficulties and our joys with—for safe relationships. This means having a place to be ourselves—our authentic selves—not having to hide behind a mask of who we really are. Loving ourselves helps us to take responsibility for what we want in life—our purpose and our goals. From this place, life provides so much more peace, joy, and happiness.

Day 60 Life is a journey

Life is a journey—it is a process! I am on a journey that varies day by day. As I learn and mature, caring for myself and loving myself changes moment by moment. I will not be perfect at it, yet I am okay with it, just as I am an okay person. I am good enough to make my own choices—to choose my mission, my purpose, and my goals. From this healthy place, I will live my life in relationship with safe others!

Reflective Meditations
Understanding My Boundaries
Photography
and Script
By Audrey Tait, MS

Contents

Introduction

Lots of people talk about boundaries. At the end of the day, it is me that has to decide what my boundaries are and how they are going to change. In the past, I may not have been aware of my boundaries. Others may have overstepped my boundaries and I did not even realize it. Anger that comes from within me is my response to someone else breaking my boundaries. I may not even be aware that my boundaries had been broken or what my boundaries were. The boundaries were still there—even unspoken. My boundaries may be too rigid or too loose. Learning more about boundaries is what this book is all about. It is in a meditative form that can be read—one a day —taking the time to think about it and reflecting on and making changes as needed. This may be new to you or you may be experienced with boundaries, there is still something that can be learned. Come with me on this journey of learning and discovering about personal boundaries.

What Are Boundaries?

Day 1 Boundaries

Boundaries are everywhere in life, although we may not realize it. Nature has many natural boundaries: the sea; land; the sun, moon, and stars in their courses; the trees and animals, how they grow and what they can do and cannot do, also the fish and birds. As a person, you also have boundaries. This may not always be obvious to you. Your skin is the boundary of your body. All your cells have boundaries. When they multiply and grow outside of their boundaries, then cancer develops. A house with locked doors is another kind of boundary; even a wall is a boundary. Think about all the physical boundaries that are around you.

Day 2 Intellectual boundaries

Beyond the physical boundaries that are more obvious to define, there are intellectual boundaries. These boundaries for humans are more than any other animal in the animal kingdom here on planet Earth. This is the higher function level of our brain. This is where our thinking brain is in the prefrontal cortex. This is the ability to learn, think, and grow in our understanding of the world around us. It is something that can be expanded in our everyday life.

Day 3 Other types of boundaries

Outside of the physical places in our world are other types of boundaries. Psychological (emotional) boundaries are harder to define. They come from within you. They are your feelings and reactions to what is going on around you. Nobody can decide your emotional boundaries. Just like your psychological boundaries are your social, spiritual, and sexual boundaries. These are also harder to define and realize due to their subjectivity; however, they are still boundaries that are a part of you.

In this book we will look at psychological (emotional) boundaries, intellectual boundaries, physical boundaries, social boundaries, spiritual boundaries, and sexual boundaries.

My Psychological (Emotional) Boundaries

Day 4 Psychological boundaries

My psychological (emotional) boundaries are all about me and how I react to what is going on in my life. I react to the self-talk that goes on in my head, to the environment around me, and to the people around me. It is all about me and how I react emotionally. There are many types of different emotions—sad, angry, numb, peaceful, joyful, hopeful, anxious, depressed, fearful, and many others. Oftentimes there is a physiological response to my emotions. So, around my psychological boundaries are how I choose to react emotionally in the minute. In times of distress, I may choose to hide my emotions until I am in a safe place to let them be expressed freely and to process them.

Day 5 Anger

Anger and the lesser form of frustration is a boundary violation. Somebody has crossed a boundary of yours, whether it is a spoken or unspoken boundary. Coming into this is also the violation of manipulation and control; these are boundary violations. It is someone trying to tell you what to do, when as an adult, you have the right to decide what you will do. It is only right that you would respond to this situation emotionally. You have the choice of what you will do with the emotion. It is also your responsibility to not hurt others in the process of dealing with your emotions.

Day 6 Trauma and emotions

When you have been affected by a big trauma, like natural disasters, wars, sexual trauma, or accidents, there is going to be emotions around the event. It may be that you go numb and cannot feel anything, or you may have a strong emotional reaction. These are emotional reactions to major events that cannot be ignored. They are major boundary violations. You need to assess the damage to know what you are dealing with. This helps you find a perspective of what is really going on. It is also knowledge that helps you put into perspective what you have to deal with in the here and now. It is easier to deal with your emotions when the unknown becomes more known. The process is not so vague.

Day 7 Ways to deal with strong emotions

There are many ways to deal with strong emotions (emotions that rage inside of you) that are safe for others and for yourself. Some ways are physical exercise, expression of emotions through artistic means (playing an instrument, painting a picture, writing in the form of journaling), talking with a safe person (family member, friend, and/or therapist), deep breathing from the diaphragm with correct posture, and sitting with the emotions until you are ready to release them. You can practice this so that when you have strong emotions in the future, you have a way to deal with them.

Day 8 Ways to deal with numbing emotions

Numbing emotions are harder to deal with.

They are hard to define and realize that there is an issue, and at some point in time they can turn from a numb emotion into a strong emotion. The best way to deal with a numb emotion, which includes low energy or feeling depressed, is breathing. If one breathes from the lungs so that the lungs expand on all sides, this brings up the energy level. You can try this and practice this so that next time you feel numb, you can use this strategy.

Day 9 Breaking others' boundaries

Breaking others' boundaries is not something that you should do. One of the things about boundaries is that you need to learn how not to break others' boundaries. You can ask someone else to do something and they have the right to decide to do it or not. You cannot force someone to do something. This would be manipulation and control. Another way of breaking someone's boundaries is by bullying. Bullying comes in all forms, including physical, sexual, and spiritual. It is your job to watch your own boundaries and not invade others' boundaries.

Day 10 An example of frustration

If someone does something that you do not like, you may or may not react to the situation and the person. The other day I was talking with a businessperson who said they did not receive what I sent them. In fact, I know they received it because the company responded to the other information that was sent in the same envelope. So, I did get frustrated. Do not try to blame me for something that is a result of someone else not doing his or her job properly. These are the types of moments in which I get to choose how I will respond. I was able to take the conversation apart after the call and see that I was indirectly being blamed for someone else's problem. This made it easier to let the issue go. I cannot change the company.

Day 11 Peace

Emotions come and go; they change in the moment, sometimes without any warning. The subconscious watches for danger and is constantly scanning the environment. This is just like animals watching for danger. We have the same responses of fight, flight, submit and feign death that we react to emotionally. Even though the subconscious is doing its duty to protect, we can learn to remain calm. The true idea in life is to strive for a place in my thoughts and emotions where there is peace and serenity in my life. When my emotions have deviated from this due to some small or big trauma, I will eventually come back to a level of calmness.

Day 12 Serenity

Serenity is the emotion or the place in life where you want to spend most of your time. It is a relaxing place that is serene, quiet, restful, and refreshing. This is the place where the soul is refreshed and you can get a sense that the world is a safe place. It takes time to be intentional and develop this state of mind. It happens more and more with practice. Part of this is allowing thoughts to enter your mind without being judgmental and condemning with your thoughts. It is also what happens to you, as you become part of your own person, believing in yourself, and trusting yourself to do what is best for you.

Day 13 Emotions part of life

Emotions are a part of your life. They are

healthy and meant to be expressed in the right place and environment. Emotions that are unhealthy need to find a way to be expressed that will not hurt others or yourself. I will practice the ways that I have learned to express my emotions so that when I have strong or numb emotions, I will know what to do.

My Intellectual Boundaries

Day 14 Intellectual boundaries

Your intellectual boundaries are for you to decide. It is your choice how you will allow others to talk to you and how you express yourself to others. This is learning to state boundaries around others and asking for them to respect your boundaries. This is also about following up the process with consequences if your boundaries are not respected. This is what the higher reasoning of your brain allows you to do.

Day 15 Brain size

Your intellectual boundaries are determined by the size of your brain. This varies from person to person. Although the parts of the brain are the same in each reasonably healthy person, our brains all function differently depending on how you have been raised. You are different from the person beside you or even a sibling. Even identical twins have some differences. The food that is eaten or taken into our bodies affects the brain and if it has the right nutrients to function properly. In other words, you are very uniquely you!

Day 16 Right-brain function

Intelligence is part of what you are good at. This varies from person to person. Right-brain function has a lot to do with the creativity of a person. Emotions also come from the right side of the brain. This is where a lot of music, art, and creative thinking come from. This may be where your talents are and it may not be where your talents are. This is a boundary issue in how your brain will affect what you do in your life for your work and your spare time. Do you function mostly from your right brain?

Day 17 Left-brain function

Another part of intelligence is the left-brain function. This is the part of the brain that is analytical. This is where a lot of thinking comes from. Depending on how this part of the brain is developed for you will determine how you use it and what you do. It may have an effect on what you do for a job and what you do in your spare time. For those who have emotions that have been shut down, this side of their brain will be more developed and they will use it more. Do you function mostly from the left brain?

Day 18 Using the intellect to control emotions

Some of the left-brain function is the ability to bring the emotions under control. This happens in different ways. One way is to name the emotions. This gets the left and right sides of the brain functioning together. It means the gear shifter in the brain needs to function between the two sides. This helps to bring the emotions under control. This is not just for strong emotions; it is also for numbing type emotions. Another way is to count to ten before speaking when in an emotional state. You can start to use your intellectual brain when your emotions start to dominate you.

Day 19 Intellectual safety

Part of your boundaries around your intelligence is not letting people put you down, not allowing the mean things they say about you to affect how you feel about yourself. Having a stop gauge means not allowing negative unfair comments about you to affect you emotionally. This means being able to make a decision of what is real and what is not real. It means assessing what is said, keeping the truth and positive comments, and letting go of the nasty, untrue statements. You can practice assessing what others say to you.

Day 20 Learning

Another part of intelligence is developing the mind—training the intellect through learning and continuing education. This can take many different forms. It does not mean that you need an education from a school system. It means learning and having a love of learning for the rest of your life, even beyond the age of retirement. This could be learning in any field that you are interested in—a hobby or career training or just something that you like to do. Today, you can choose to learn something new.

Day 21 Your intelligence

Your intelligence involves a number of aspects of your life. It is to be cherished and used to the best of your ability. It is to be stimulated to grow and change with lifelong learning. It is to be used to have a choice in how you express your emotions. Your intelligence is yours to cherish.

My Physical Boundaries

Day 22 Boundaries

Your physical boundaries are determined by the physical makeup of your body. Your body is unique; there is no one else who has the same genetic DNA code that you have unless you are an identical twin. Even twins are somewhat different. There are assets that most people have and then there are limitations. For me, I have issues with low blood sugar; this is not diabetes. I have to be concerned with the balance of energy input and output, meaning how much and when I eat with physical activity. Doing vigorous exercise three to four hours after a meal will probably mean that my blood sugar will go low and I will have a hard time thinking. To compensate for this, I make sure that I have a healthy snack with me so that I can eat, if necessary. What are your physical limitations with your body?

Day 23 Physical being as boundaries

Your physical body is a boundary; my skin is the boundary between me and the world around me. You did not choose your physical body, the sex that you were at birth, the genetic code that your body is made up of, or the epigenetics at birth (the expression of your genes in the past couple of generations), your skin color, your height, your hair or eye color, or your nationality. These are all boundaries that you did not choose. These are boundaries that you can accept or reject. Do you accept your body makeup?

Day 24 Physical limitations as boundaries

Physical limitations are boundaries. These limitations must be dealt with and managed. Diabetes requires proper nutrition, exercise, and maintaining correct blood sugar level. Other health problems demand attention and are limitations of what you can and cannot do. Management is an individual choice.

What works for you may not work for another person with the same physical issue, as each person's body is different. You can choose to manage your physical limitations.

Day 25 Physical assets as boundaries

On the other hand, there are physical assets to a body. The tall male has an advantage over the short male when it comes to playing basketball. Some musicians have perfect pitch and others have relative pitch. The short woman may be more attractive to the tall male. Some bodies appear more sexual than others. So, you may have physical assets to your body. What physical assets do you have?

Day 26 Self-care as a boundary

Self-care is something that is extremely important. Self-care is taking care of your body, mind, and soul. Someone else cannot do it for you. You have to do it for yourself. You need to eat your own food, drink your own water, go to the bathroom yourself, and so the list goes on. You are responsible for yourself even if you are part of a family or a group. Will you take care of yourself?

Day 27 Trauma

Trauma affects the brain and and functioning at the high level of reasoning. Trauma tends to turn off the reasoning of the brain in the moment, making it harder to think straight in the moment. This is a physical part of the way the brain works. This can be changed over time by deep breathing from the diaphragm, lying on the stomach so that the deep breathing will come automatically, or standing up to get the thinking brain on board to calm the system down. What will you practice today?

Day 28 Addictions

Addictions affect the physical body. If the addiction is a substance that is put into the body, then there is a direct effect on the body. This varies depending on the substance. If the substance is a process addiction, such as workaholism, disordered eating, sexual addiction, or gambling, then the body is still affected. The brain is still affected like it is by a substance. There is a choice at first and then it becomes a non-choice. One cannot stop the addiction and one needs more of it to get the same effect. Addictions tend to arrest the character development at the age that the addiction starts, keeping a person stuck at that age level for character development. This is like a dry drunk who is not pleasant to be around. An addiction is a boundary issue with the self. Are you addicted to anything that is affecting your physical boundaries?

Day 29 How to improve

Improving your physical body is something that you can do through exercise and bodybuilding. You may need to see a physician before you start a program. This is an area that you have a choice about. You can be a couch potato or you can be physically fit. Being physically fit helps you deal with whatever happens in life. Do you want to be physically fit?

Day 30 Physical body

Your physical body has limitations and assets that determine, to a certain extent, what you are physically capable of. These are the things that you did not choose and cannot change. You can become healthier and be proactive in making changes that will allow you to become the person you want to become. What are your choices today?

My Social Boundaries

Day 31 Social boundaries

Social boundaries are those boundaries that are around you in your social relationships. This includes your relationships with family, friends, and work associates. The list goes on really to include anyone you meet, even people you pass in the street. The boundaries are what you will and will not do and tolerate. If you want to stop and talk to someone, you can or if you want to avoid that person, you can. This is all about the boundaries that you make in your relationship.

Day 32 Individuation

The goal of everyone in life is to become an individual in themselves, to individuate. As one grows, there is a change from being a part of the mother as a baby to becoming an individual. This happens through the growing up years. Usually this is completed sometime in the teen years. Many things can keep this from happening—enmeshment in the family, the rigid family, the overcontrolling or manipulating parents who do not allow the child to become the person they were mean to be. Sometimes becoming an individual does not happen until later in life. The idea is to become your own person, to figure out "who you are, what you like, who you want to become, and how you want to relate to others." It is the "real you" inside of you. If you are afraid of what others will think of you if they really knew you, then you may be the only person who ever really knows you. When this happens, other people do not know your authentic self. The goal in becoming an individual is to become authentic in all parts of your life.

Day 33 Alone time

With social time, there is the social time with self. The amount of this time will vary depending on if you are an introvert or an extrovert. When you become authentic and heal the disappointments, discouragements, and trauma from the past, it is easier to be by oneself—to sit and enjoy a cup of tea in a relaxing environment. There is the time that you can spend in meditation. For the single person living alone, there is the time in the middle of the night when you cannot sleep. As you learn to be yourself, this time becomes time that one does not fear or avoid; it becomes times when one gets to grow and be refreshed. These are the boundaries that you can develop around yourself and not always be dependent on others.

Day 34 Together time

Together time with others will also depend on the type of person you are—extrovert or introvert. This is where boundaries are important. It does not matter who you are around, there needs to be boundaries in every relationship. Boundaries include the amount of time you spend together, where you spend it, who you spend it with, how you will spend the time, and why you will spend the time together. Each of these elements is a boundary. The boundaries need to be flexible and change in a dynamic relationship. If there is an emergency that I am called to, then I need to stop what I am doing and attend to the emergency. Maybe the present moment of being together will happen at a later date.

Day 35 Family associations

Family associations can be tricky. You did not choose your grandparents, your parents, your siblings, and how you are treated by these people. Some families seem to have it all together. They seem to be secure individuals and groups of people. And yet what it seems like on the outside is not always what it is on the inside behind closed doors. Then, there are others who are not allowed to become individuals because there is rigidity or enmeshment in the family. Some of the old sayings like "If you want to cry, I will give you a reason to cry," "Children are to be seen and not heard," "No, you did not want that you wanted this," and so the list goes on. These sayings have not allowed people to become authentic individuals. Perhaps your family is very different. This is where one needs to develop boundaries around family. Your boundaries may welcome certain members of the family and have restrictions on others. As times change, your boundaries can also change. Family is one of the more difficult areas to have social boundaries.

Day 36 Friend associations

Relationships with friends are different from family associations. You get to choose who you want to associate with. When one relationship is not working and it is a one-way give, you always giving to the other person and the other person not giving back, then you may want to consider putting boundaries around the relationship with consequences or ending the relationship. On the other hand, if the two of you both like the relationship and want to continue it, then developing it and spending time together is worth the effort. This again is a boundary issue of how you handle the situation. You have choices with your relationships.

Day 37 Business associations

Business associations are trickier than relationships with friends. These are the people you work with and spend a lot of time with—depending on what you do for a living. There are possibly times where you want to argue with a boss who is very unsupportive. Leaving the situation is not always possible. This is where finding other ways to deal with the situation is possible. For example, having other safe people who can support you, journaling to get the strong feelings out of the soul, and other ways to de-escalate the emotions. Then, there are the people at work that you associate with. This is where you need to have boundaries around what you do and do not talk about. If you want to tell all about your life, this may not be the safe place to do it. This is where having friends in other places to help you is a must.

Day 38 Safety first

In all relationships—social or otherwise—safety comes first. If there are issues around verbal, emotional, physical, mental, spiritual, or sexual abuse in any form, there needs to be boundaries around it followed up by consequences. When assault is happening, do what is best in the moment—fight, flight, freeze, submit, or scream. Then afterward get the help that you need to deal with the event. Do not wait for years for the effects of the trauma to take its toll on you or on your body—physically, emotionally, and socially. Get help now!

Day 39 Social relationships

Social relationships can be tricky and yet they can be an inspiration to your life. You need boundaries around your relationships to keep you healthy, to help you be the person you are meant to be, and to be your authentic self. Recently, I was offered a place to stay overnight and refused it because I did not know the people and it was my boundary issue. What areas of your social life do you need to put boundaries around?

Day 40 What spirituality is

Spirituality in the context of this book is finding a relationship with a Higher Power, with the God of your understanding. This is not a religious organization or a series of religious beliefs. This is about finding your inner voice, that voice that speaks to you. It's about finding emotional release so you can sit by yourself and be comfortable and listen to that voice. This is about finding your purpose in life, what you were meant to do, and what path you were meant to take in this life.

Day 41 A relationship

Relationships come and go in life. There are relationships with family—parents, spouses, children, and other relatives—friends, and acquaintances; then there are relationships with those at work and other businesses. The most important relationship is with the self. This is where we get into a lot of trouble as we judge and shame ourselves, take messages—overt and covert from others—and change them to all the negative reactions possible. It is the stilling of the judgments and shame that allow for peace and serenity to come into my life—an accepting of the self. Then, there is the opportunity to listen to the inner voice to find your vision in life and your path. Will you choose to and continue to love yourself?

Day 42 God of your understanding

The God of your understanding is different for everyone. We are all at different places in our journey of life. This is not a time to think I am better than the other person. They are just at a different stage of their journey. The thing to remember is that we all start out with a different set of circumstances. Some come from secure families and other from insecure families; this all has an effect on how one starts and lives life—more serenity in infancy and childhood mean a calmer life. We still have the option to develop a calmer, more peaceful life. This all has an effect on the God of our understanding. What is your understanding of God?

Day 43 Religious organizations

This is not to disagree with any religious organization. The issue that comes in life is that many have been abused by such organizations. This abuse could be physical, sexual, or any other kind of possible abuse. The abuse that is rarely addressed is spiritual abuse. This can be just as devastating as the other kinds of abuse. It keeps people from going back to that religious organization and at time takes away their support system. The idea here is to take that time to find the inner peace and healing that comes with the self. This takes time. Then when one is ready, it may be possible to return to the previous organization. This is all about boundaries. If one returns, then what are my boundaries if something happens again? Will I arrive there so that I have access to leave if I need to? Will I go with a safe person who will leave whenever I need to leave? I can decide whom I will and will not talk to ahead of time. I can be cautious of where I sit, stand, or walk so as to avoid others if needed. If there has been physical or sexual abuse, then I may need to find another place to attend. Today, I will learn to make proactive choice of my involvement in religious organizations that I will be involved in.

Day 44 Emotional release

The emotional release is what comes in forgiveness or letting go. It is letting go of the negative emotions that go around in your head that take up your time and keep you stuck from moving forward. It is these emotions that you need to release. This comes with time. You can release them faster by practicing the healing techniques in Reflective Meditations: Healing My Trauma. *Letting go of these emotions does not mean forgetting what happened, not holding the other person to boundaries and consequences, or a guarantee of reconciliation or restitution. The emotional release is strictly for you and your emotional well-being. You can start the process or continue the process of releasing strong emotions.*

Day 45 Inner voice

That inner voice is the voice that you can hear when you still your mind in a quiet place. Even before you learn to still your mind, that voice is still there. It is the voice that is encouraging and leading you down a path of serenity. It is a task to develop the ability to hear this inner voice. It comes with practice and time. You can practice releasing small frustrations so that you can develop the ability to listen to that still, small inner voice.

Day 46 Purpose

Finding one's purpose in life is part of the tasks of life of becoming an individual. When you become whole in yourself without needing the assurance of others, then it is easier to find your purpose. Finding your purpose comes from looking at the past. Your greatest strength is found in your greatest difficulty—not something that we want to understand or admit to. However, looking at your story you can usually find what your purpose is. This will take time. For me, the author, my background of abuse has taken me on a path of experience and training so that I can help others with what was helpful for me. You can assess your life to find your own purpose.

Day 47 Path

When I know my purpose, then it is easier to determine a path. Questions start to come up like, "Do I need more education or training?" "What are my passions?" "How can I make a difference?" Having a five-year plan is a place to start this process. Once I have the plan, then I can start determining my goals. The idea is to realize that this is just a template and things may not go exactly as planned. So, this goes back to the acceptance of what is happening in my life—of not judging myself negatively and being accepting of the process. You can start the process of planning your path, including your spiritual path.

Day 48 Spiritual boundaries

Spiritual boundaries come in many shapes and sizes. The first really starts with a letting go of the emotional trauma that occupies my mind and keeps me stuck from being the person I was meant to be. This allows me to find the inner voice—that still small voice that is within me. This allows me to find my purpose and my path in life. What an awesomeness that can happen from this process. Today, although how difficult this process may be, I will start or continue down the path of finding myself, my purpose, and my path.

My Sexual Boundaries

Day 49 The idea of sexual boundaries

The idea of sexual boundaries in our day and age, especially for the young, is not something that one wants to think about. Everything is so free in our society—a total difference from a couple of generations ago. The reality is still the same; even with very loose ideas around sex and actual practice, there is still a limit to what one will do, spoken or unspoken. You still have boundaries. You get to determine what your boundaries are.

Day 50 Sexual and spiritual boundaries

One of the places that sexual boundaries clash is with spiritual (religious) beliefs. The reality that sex is in the brain is becoming very evident these days. To avoid a lot of confusion, guilt, and negative self-talk, it makes sense to spend some time figuring out where your spiritual and sexual boundaries cross—where they come together, where they meet, where you want them to be—so that you are not self-critical because you crossed your own boundaries. This may not be an issue for you and not take any time to think about; for others this may take days to make a decision, with the need to do so serious thinking and possibly research. You can take the time to explore your spiritual and your sexual boundaries.

Day 51 Stating what I want

Within a sexual relationship that is right for you, you have the right to say "no" to sex at any time. If you do not like what your partner is doing, it is your responsibility to state or express "I do not like that." On the other hand, if you really like something, it is your choice to let your partner know "I really like that." Maybe you want to try it again by saying, "Can you do that again, please." The reality is that your partner cannot read your mind; you need to tell that person what you like. This is your responsibility. You can let your partner know what you like.

Day 52 Exploring sex

To find what I like and do not like when it comes to sex takes time to explore. It is not a onetime event; it is a discovery process that never ends. Today, you might find something new and it may be months before you find something new again—it is still a discovery process. You may find something by accident, or you may find something by intentionally exploring what you really like. You can take the time to explore your own sexuality.

Day 53 What is sex?

Sex is more than the act of intercourse. It includes all the foreplay and explorations that happens before the climax. This is another area of discovery that you can spend time on. For the single person who is not married, sex is more than just the foreplay and sexual intercourse. The reality is that sex is an express of the self. It can be expression in music, art, dance, painting, and any creative expression. So, when exploring sex for any person, it is exploring the creative side of the brain or the expression of the person. You can explore your creativity.

Day 54 What is healthy sex?

Asking the question "What is healthy sex?" is a good question. Healthy sex will be different for everyone. Part of this will be determined by your relationship between sexual and spiritual beliefs. For the person for whom sex is compulsive and out of control, healthy sex will need to be something that is not out of control. For the person who does not like sex or is afraid of sex, their healthy sexuality will need to include boundaries that allow for growth in a healthy way. For the person who is secure in a sexual relationship, maybe their healthy boundaries need to include some variations to stimulate growth. You can spend time determining what is healthy sexuality for yourself. You can find your boundaries now in the current time and allow your sexual boundaries to adapt and change over time in a healthy way.

Day 55 Healthy sexuality continued

Usually, healthy sexually is in a committed relationship. It includes foreplay and intercourse. There are other types of sexual encounters that may or may not be right for you in this relationship. This is where there is some flexibility on what you like and what you do not like. For those who are single, you need to determine what healthy sexuality will look like for you within your belief system. Will it be expressing the creative side that you have or will it include more? What is healthy sexuality for you?

Day 56 Abused sexual boundaries

One cannot talk about sex without talking about sexual abuse, sexual molestation, and rape. These are sad facts in life that many, especially woman, are affected by. Healing takes a long time psychologically, mentally, and sexually. If this is your issue, then you need to find a safe place that you can talk about this in your culture.

Day 57 Sexual boundaries

Sexual boundaries are still a type of boundary that needs to be determined by you. Your spiritual beliefs will be a part of determining your spiritual boundaries. The reality is that spirituality and sexuality grow together. If one is stunted, so will the other be stunted. If one is growing and changing in a dynamic relationship, so will the other. You get to choose how you will grow both spiritually and sexually.

Where to Go from Here

Day 58 Boundaries

Boundaries are part of our life in every area of our life. There is not a part of life that does not have boundaries. Some are more obvious than others, while some are more subjective. Some boundaries need to be rigid and never change like the shores of seas, lakes, river, and ponds—otherwise we end up with floods. Other boundaries, like our own boundaries, need to be changing and flexible to deal with the situation in the moment. Boundaries around abuse and rape need to be rigid to keep those around us safe. You still get to decide what your boundaries are going to be.

Day 59 Safe boundaries

The idea of having boundaries is to make your life safer for you—to keep trauma from happening or to keep it to a minimal effect on you and to keep you and those around you, especially those who are dependent on you, safe. This is to bring more peace, love, joy, and serenity into your life. May this be your life.

Day 60 From here

From here is the everyday practice of continuing to learn and grow your own boundaries. It is a process that is never ending. What works today may not work tomorrow and may need to be changed. What does not work needs to be followed up with consequences. This takes it one step further, letting the other person know that you mean what you say. May you continue on this journey of boundaries and may it be a pleasant one for you, keeping you safe.

Further Reading

Reflective Meditations Trilogy:
Understanding My Trauma,
Healing My Trauma,
and
Letting Go–Forgiveness!
Script and photography by Audrey Tait, MS

I Am Wonderfully Me:
Positive Affirmations for Me!
Volume 1-3
Script and photography by Audrey Tait, MS

About the Author

Audrey Tait has a love of photography and has a master's degree in Addiction Counselling and a bachelor's degree in Dietetics. She is a Canadian Certified Counsellor; Certified Sex Addiction Therapist, candidate; Certified Multiple Addiction Therapist, candidate; and Registered Dietitian, Alberta, Canada. In addition, she is a member of the Canadian Counselling and Psychotherapy Association; College of Dietitians of Alberta; and the Alpha Chi Honors Society. She has specialized training in trauma, character, and developmental issues along with cognitive therapy. She is owner/ president of Inspirational Insights Counselling, Inc., where therapy is offered to those seeking a deeper meaning in life.

www.inspirationalinsightcounselling.com

www.ingramcontent.com/pod-product-compliance
Ingram Content Group UK Ltd.
Pitfield, Milton Keynes, MK11 3LW, UK
UKHW060020051026
15591UKWH00006B/295